Encyclopedia
of Private Capital
Markets

(Quick Reference)

Craig R. Everett, PhD

FISCAL PRESS

Notices
This work attempts to identify and define commonly used terms in private capital markets. These terms are constantly changing and being added upon, and definitions of these terms may not be consistent across the industry. Thus, the reader must use this work at their own risk. The author and publisher are not responsible for any financial damages due to misunderstandings about deal terms or valuations discussed in this work.

Product names and corporate names mentioned in this work may be trademarks and are used only for identification and explanation without intent to infringe.

Publisher's Cataloging-in-Publication Data
Everett, Craig R.
   Encyclopedia of Private Capital Markets (Quick Reference) / by Craig R. Everett. – p. cm.

ISBN 978-0-9882374-4-5 (pbk.)
1. Capital Investments. 2. Corporations. 3. Private Companies-Finance. I. Title.
HG4751
332'.6-dc23

Library of Congress Control Number: 2016903317
ISBN: 978-0-9882374-4-5 (paperback)
ISBN: 978-0-9882374-5-2 (e-book)

Fiscal Press
2629 Townsgate Road Suite 235
Westlake Village, CA 91361

CONTENTS

FORWARD AND ACKNOWLEDGEMENTS

Finance professionals new to doing private company deals have a tremendous learning curve with respect to the complex industry jargon. The Encyclopedia of Private Capital Markets (Quick Reference) is intended to readers come up to speed quickly. It is written in dictionary format in order to provide easy access.

This material was written primarily as a resource for my own graduate business students at Pepperdine, but it is my hope that it will prove to be useful to a much broader audience. Essentially, this is a "quick reference" that is a condensed version of the longer and larger Encyclopedia of Private Capital Markets (a.k.a. "EPCM"). The primary difference is that the full EPCM, in addition to definitions, also contains explanations and examples. At the time of the publication of this quick reference (QR), the full EPCM is still a work-in-progress and is not yet publicly available.

I would particularly like to thank Rob Slee, author of the seminal book, "Private Capital Markets: Valuation, Capitalization, and Transfer of Private Business Interests". With his permission, I have included many of his terms and phrases. Rob Slee is the pioneer of the entire field of private capital markets. I would also like to thank Dr. John Paglia, who is the founder of the Pepperdine Private Capital Markets Project. The industry is constantly changing, so this is a work-in-progress. New private capital words, phrases and acronyms appear every year, which means that this guide will never be truly finished. If you notice any errors or deficiencies, please let me know.

- Craig R. Everett, PhD

  craig.everett@gmail.com

Part I

Alphabetical Listing
of all Terms

Valuation Terms

Adjusted Indicated Value
Value conclusion after any discounts or premiums are applied.

Appraisal
An estimate of the value of a company. See Valuation.

Appraisal Remedy
Dissenter's rights statutes that serve to protect the minority, typically through the purchase of their stock at fair value.

Appraisal Standards
Standards that provide structure for the practice of valuation.

ASA
Accredited Senior Appraiser.

Asset Approach
Method of valuation that uses the underlying assets and net liabilities of a business to derive a value.

Before and After Method
Method of valuation that compares the revenues and profits before and after the business interruption.

Beta
A measure of systematic risk of a security; the tendency of a security's returns to correlate with swings in the broad market.

Black-Scholes
A model for pricing call options that uses the stock price, the exercise price, the risk-free interest rate, the time to expiration, and the standard deviation of the historical return of the underlying stock.

Brand Equity
The monetary value of having a well-known brand.

Build-Up Method
Used by professional appraisers to calculate a discount rate. Generally starts with the risk-free rate and then premiums are added to it to arrive at an overall cost of capital.

Business Valuation
The act or process of determining the value of a business enterprise or ownership interest therein.

Capital Asset Pricing Model (CAPM)
An economic theory that describes the relationship between risk and expected return, and serves as a model for the pricing of risky securities.

Capital Budget
A firm's set of planned capital expenditures.

Capitalization Rate
Any divisor used to convert a benefit stream into value.

Capitalize
To convert a benefit stream into a value.

Cash Flow
Cash that is generated over a period of time by an asset, group of assets, or business enterprise.

Company-Specific Risk
The portion of total risk specific to an individual security that can be avoided through diversification. See Idiosyncratic Risk or Unsystematic Risk

Control Premium
An amount by which the pro rata value of a controlling interest exceeds the pro rata value of a noncontrolling interest in a business enterprise that reflects the power of control.

Copyright
A form of legal protection used to safeguard original literary works, performing arts, sound recordings, visual arts, original software code and renewals. Protected for the life of the author plus 70 years.

Cost Approach
Measures future benefits of ownership and amount of money necessary to replace its future service capabilities.

Cost of Capital
The expected rate of return that a market requires in order to attract funds to a particular investment.

Cost of Equity
The expected rate of return that an Individual investor requires in order to attract funds to a particular investment.

Cost Savings Synergy
Synergy that results from expenses that are no longer needed when business functions are consolidated.

Depreciation
A non-cash charge that reduces the accounting value of fixed assets due to wear, age or obsolescence.

Depreciation Tax Shield
The value of the tax write-off on depreciation of plant and equipment.

Design Patent
Protects the original appearance of an article of manufacture, not its structural features. Carries a term of 14 years.

Direct Valuation
Value is determined by direct reference to actual comparable data.

Discount
A reduction in value or the act of reducing value. In finance refers to calculating the present value of a future cash flow using a discount rate (cost of capital). Discounting is the opposite of compounding.

Discount Rate
The expected rates of return that investors require in order to attract funds to a particular investment. See Cost of Capital.

Discounted Cash Flow (DCF)
Finding the present value of an opportunity by calculating the sum of discounted expected future cash flows.

Discretionary Earnings
The amount of a company's income available for spending after the essentials have been met.

Done Deals
Database collected from all SEC filings of acquisition transactions.

Early Equity Value
The value of a business interest as a startup, often prior to profit or even revenue.

Earning Capacity
The future profit picture of a firm.

Earnings Before Interest and Taxes (EBIT)
The figure for operating income after depreciation but without allowing for debt service or what is owed to the government for taxes.

Earnings Before Interest, Taxes, Depreciation and Amor
Earnings before interest, taxes, depreciation, and amortization.

Economic Life
The period of time over which property may generate economic benefits. Often the amount of time a piece of equipment is expected to last.

Economic Value
Measurement of generating a return in excess of the corresponding cost of capital.

Enterprise Value
Value of 100% of the ownership.

Equity Risk Premium
The amount that investors are compensated for assuming nondiversifiable equity risk.

Excess Earnings
That amount of anticipated benefits that exceeds a fair rate of return on the value of a selected asset base (often net tangible assets) used to generate those anticipated benefits.

Expected Future Cash Flows
Projected future cash flows associated with an asset of decision.

Expected Rate of Return
The rate of return expected on an investment by the capital provider.

Explicit Weighting
The assignment of percentage weights to different methods of valuation for stated reasons.

Fair Market Value
The price at which the property would change hands between a willing buyer and a willing seller when the buyer is not under any compulsion to buy and the seller is not under any compulsion to sell, and both parties having reasonable knowledge of relevant

Fair Valuation Date
Date before the effectuation of the corporate action to which the dissenter objects.

Fair Value
The value of the shares immediately before a corporate action to which the dissenter objects, excluding any appreciation or depreciation in anticipation of the corporate action unless exclusion would be inequitable.

Fair Value (FASB definition)
The amount at which an asset (or liability) could be bought (or incurred) or sold (or settled) in a current transaction between willing parties, that is, other than in a forced or liquidation sale.

Financial Control Premium
Control value of an enterprise based on financial returns.

Forced Liquidation Value
Estimated gross amount of money that could be realized from sale in public auction, or negotiated liquidation sale with seller having a sense of immediacy.

Free Cash Flow
Net income plus non-cash charges to income, specifically depreciation and amortization less capital expenditures, to sustain the basic business.

Function
The specific use of an appraisal, which leads directly to the choice of appropriate methods to employ.

Future Value
The amount of money that an investment made today (the present value) will grow to by some future date. Since money has time value, we naturally expect the future value to be greater than the present value. The difference between the two depends on the number of compounding periods involved and the interest rate.

Going Concern
An ongoing operating business enterprise

Going Concern Assumption
Assumption that a business will remain in operation indefinitely.

Going Concern Value
The value of a business enterprise that is expected to continue to operate into the future.

Hurdle Rate
The required return in capital budgeting. Specifically, the minimum expected IRR that a venture would require to be approved.

Idiosyncratic Risk
The portion of total risk specific to an individual security that can be avoided through diversification. See Unsystematic Risk or Company-Specific Risk

Implicit Weighting
The weighting of a value conclusion based on the adjusted indicated values of various valuation methods.

Income Approach
Method of valuation that ultimately converts anticipated benefits into a present value.

Incremental Business Value (IBV)
A measure of how much value that management has added to the company. IBV = Recast EBITDA - (Investment x private cost of capital).

Indirect Valuation
Value is determined using a method that indirectly estimates value.

Institute of Business Appraisers (IBA)
The oldest business appraisal society in the U. S.

Insurable Value
One of a number of appropriate values that may be used to determine the funding amount for a buy/sell agreement or the value sought for determining the necessary amount of insurance coverage or claim.

Intangible Assets
Non-physical assets (such as franchises, trademarks, patents, copyrights, goodwill, equities, mineral rights, securities, and contracts as distinguished from physical assets) that grant rights, privileges, and have economic benefits for the owner.

Intellectual Assets
Intangible assets particular to a company that add to the enterprise value.

Intellectual Capital
The sum of Human Capital and Structural Capital.

Intellectual Property
An original idea or concept of the creator that can be trademarked, patented, copyrighted, or held as a trade secret.

Interest Tax Shield
The reductions in income taxes that result from the tax-deductibility of interest payments.

Internal Rate of Return
Discount rate at which investment has a net present value equal to zero.

Invested Capital
The sum of equity and debt in a business enterprise.

Investment Value
The value of a business interest to a particular investor.

IRS Published Interest Rate
Benchmark interest rate set forth by the IRS.

Key Person
Important person without whom a company can expect to experience a decrease in future income.

Key Person Discount
An amount or percentage deducted from the value of an ownership interest to reflect the reduction in value resulting from the actual or potential loss of a key person in a business enterprise.

Lack of Marketability Discount
An amount or percentage deducted from the value of an ownership interest to reflect the relative absence of marketability.

Levered Beta
The beta reflecting a capital structure that includes debt.

Lifestyle Business
Firms that are not seeking value maximization as a primary objective.

Liquidation Value
Net amount that could be realized by selling the assets of a firm after repaying the debt. Value of a firm in dissolution.

Liquidity
The amount and ease by which an asset can be converted to cash. Frequently measure by the current ratio.

Lost Profits
Commercial damages due to a business interruption.

Marginal Cost of Capital
The firm's incremental cost of capital associated with its next dollar of total new financing.

Market Approach
Method of valuation that compares the subject to similar businesses, business ownership interests, securities, or intangible assets that have been sold.

Market Capitalization
The total dollar value of all outstanding shares. Computed as shares times current market price. It is a measure of corporate size.

Market Value
The highest purchase price available in the marketplace for selected assets or stock of the company.

Marketability
The ability to quickly convert property to cash at minimal cost. See Liquidity.

Mean
The expected value of a random variable.

Median
The value of the midpoint variable when the data are arranged in ascending or descending order.

Minority Discount
A discount for lack of control applicable to a minority interest.

Monte Carlo Simulation
An analytical technique for solving a problem by performing a large number of trail runs, called simulations, and inferring a solution from the collective results of the trial runs. Method for calculating the probability distribution of possible outcomes.

NACVA
National Association of Certified Valuation Analysts.

Net Asset Value
The adjustment of a company's assets and liabilities to market values.

Net Present Value (NPV)
The present value of the expected future cash flows minus the cost.

Non-Advocacy
Stance of indifference an appraiser must take in order to conduct a fair and unbiased appraisal.

Opportunity Cost of Capital
Expected return that is foregone by investing in a project rather than in comparable financial securities.

Orderly Liquidation Value
Estimated gross amount of money that could be realized from a sale, given reasonable time to find purchasers, with the seller being compelled to sell as is.

Overhead
The costs associated with providing and maintaining a manufacturing or working environment that cannot be traced directly to the production or sale of identifiable goods and services.

Patent
The grant of a property right by the U.S. government to the inventor by action of the Patent and Trademark office.

Payback Period
The length of time it takes to recover the initial cost of a project, without regard to the time value of money.

Point-In-Time Value
Appraised value of a private firm at a particular point-in-time.

Portfolio Discount
An amount or percentage that may be deducted from the value of a business enterprise to reflect the fact that it owns dissimilar operations or assets that may not fit well together.

Post-Money Valuation
The "pre-money" valuation of the company plus the amount of the investment.

Pratt's Stats
Official database of the International Business Brokers
Association. Covers acquisitions in the $1-30 million range and
details over seventy different data fields per transaction.

Pre-IPO Studies
Conducted to determine a stock's marketability discount upon
initial offering.

Pre-Money Valuation
Value of a company prior to accepting further investment.

Present Value
The value today of a future payment, or stream of payments,
discounted at some appropriate interest rate.

Principle of Substitution
Value is determined by the cost of acquiring an equally desirable
substitute.

Private Guideline Search
Method that uses comparable acquisitions, analyzes them, and
attempts to derive a value decision based on the information
gathered.

Probability-weighted Analysis
Incorporating expectations about possible variation in the amount
or timing of cash flows into an analysis.

Proportionate Interests
Notion that dissenting shareholders have the right to see their
equity stake valued on a going concern basis rather than a
liquidation basis.

Public Guideline Companies
Public companies used in the valuation of a private company due
to the comparative qualities between them.

Recast EBIT
Recast earnings before interest and taxes.

Recast EBITDA
Recast earnings before interest, taxes, depreciation, and amortization.

Replacement Cost New
The current cost of a similar new property having the nearest equivalent utility to the property being valued.

Report Date
The date conclusions are transmitted to the client.

Reporting Unit
In impaired goodwill, an operating division for which management has reviewed and assessed performance.

Residual Value
Value remaining in equipment after lease term has expired.

Restricted Stock Studies
Examine the issuance of restricted common stock of companies with actively traded public shares.

Revenue Ruling 59-60
U.S. Treasury Department ruling that outlines procedures for determining fair market value of private companies.

Risk-free Rate
The rate earned on a riskless asset. Technically not measurable, but in practice, US Treasury securities such as the 10-year treasury bond are used as a proxy for the risk-free rate.

Rule of Thumb
A mathematical relationship between or among variables based on experience, observation, hearsay, or a combination of these, usually applicable to a specific industry.

Run Rate
The financial performance of a company if current results are extrapolated over a certain period of time.

Salvage Value
Scrap value of plant and equipment.

Schilt Risk Premium Matrix
Determines the discount rate by adding a risk-free rate with a premium that is associated with different levels of risk.

Shared Control Value
Level where no block of ownership has more than 50% of the shares.

Size Premium
The amount that investors are compensated for assuming diversifiable or company specific risk.

Standard of Value
The identification of the type of value being utilized in a specific engagement.

Strategic Control Value
Value of 100% of the company based on strategic or synergistic considerations.

Structural Capital
The hardware, software, databases, organizational structure, and everything else of organizational capability that supports employee productivity.

Sunk Costs
Costs that have been incurred and cannot be reversed.

Synergy
The increase in performance of the combined firm over what the two firms are expected to accomplish as independent companies.

Systematic Risk
The risk common to all securities that cannot be eliminated through diversification. When using the capital asset pricing model systematic risk is measured by beta.

Tangible asset
An asset whose value depends on particular physical properties.

Technical Know How
Proficiency in computers and/or other forms of applicable technology.

Terminal Value
The value as of the end of the discrete projection period in a discounted benefit stream model.

Terms Cost
Cost of a financing beyond the stated interest rate.

Time Value of Money
The concept that money available today is worth more than that same amount in the future.

Trade Secrets
Any proprietary technology not generally known in the trade.

Trademarks
Protected word, name, symbol, or device or combination thereof used by a company to identify and distinguish its goods from competitors. Carries a term of 10 years, renewable upon expiration.

Unadjusted Indicated Value
Value conclusion before any discounts or premiums are applied.

Unlevered Beta
The beta reflecting the risk of a firm if it had a capital structure without debt.

Unsystematic Risk
The portion of total risk specific to an individual security that can be avoided through diversification. See Idiosyncratic Risk or Company-Specific Risk

USPAP
Uniform Standards of Professional Appraisal Practice.

Utility Patents
Patent on an invention or any certifiable improvement of an existing product. Carry a term of 20 years from date of application.

Valuation
The act or process of determining the value of a business, business ownership interest, security, or intangible asset.

Valuation Approach
A general way of determining a value indication of a business, business ownership interest, security, or intangible asset using one or more valuation methods.

Valuation Date
The specific point in time as of which the valuator's opinion of value applies (also referred to as "Effective Date" or "Appraisal Date").

Valuation Method
Within approaches, a specific way to determine value.

Value Conclusion
Ultimate value after all adjustments are applied.

Weighted Cost of Capital (WACC)
The expected return on a portfolio of all a firm's equity and debt securities. Used as a hurdle rate for capital investment.

Write-down
Decreasing the book value of an asset if its book value is overstated compared to current market values.

Yardstick Approach
Valuation method that makes a comparison with similar businesses to determine if there is a difference in the level of the plaintiff's performance after a business interruption.

Business & Economics Terms

Agency Theory
The analysis of potential conflicts in principal-agent relationships, wherein one person, an agent, acts on behalf of another person, a principal.

Agent
The decision-maker in a principal-agent relationship. The agent represents the interests of the principal.

AICPA
American Institute of Certified Public Accountants. The world's largest association of accountants, setting ethical standards, lobbying and providing the CPA exam.

Allocation
Market process of rationing resources.

Arm's Length Price
The price at which a willing buyer and a willing unrelated seller would freely agree to transact.

ASA
Accredited Senior Appraiser.

Asymmetric Information
Information known to some people but not to other people.

Auction Markets
Markets in which the prevailing price is determined through the free interaction of prospective buyers and sellers, as on the floor of the stock exchange.

Bulletin Board
Electronic quotation system that displays real-time quotes, last sale prices, and volume information for many over the counter stocks.

Business Cycle
Ongoing process of booms and busts in the life of a business or the economy.

Business Enterprise
A commercial, industrial, service, or investment entity, or a combination thereof, pursuing economic activity.

Business Interruption
External event that hurts the prospective earnings of a company by impeding its operations.

Capital Asset Pricing Model (CAPM)
An economic theory that describes the relationship between risk and expected return, and serves as a model for the pricing of risky securities.

Capital Efficiency
Maximizing returns while employing the least amount of capital possible. Often measured by Return on Capital Employed (ROCE).

Capital Structure
The mix of debt and equity financing in a business.

Capital Types
The six broad categories of capital available in the private capital markets. They include bank lending, equipment leasing, asset based lending, factoring, mezzanine debt, and private equity.

Capitalization
The process of forming capital structure through risk and return assessments or the conversion of a benefit stream to a present value.

Channel Expansion
Growing sales through the exploitation of new distribution approaches.

Company-Specific Risk
The portion of total risk specific to an individual security that can be avoided through diversification. See Idiosyncratic Risk or Unsystematic Risk

Compounded Rate of Return
The rate of return on an investment where reinvestment of the cash flows increases the yield.

Compounding
The process of accumulating the time value of money forward in time.

Consolidation
A period where there is intensive merger activity within an industry resulting in a measurably reduced number of firms in that industry.

Corporate Finance
The study of the manner in which companies make investment and financing decisions.

Cost of Capital
The expected rate of return that a market requires in order to attract funds to a particular investment.

Credit Box
The qualification boundaries that must be met in order to qualify for a particular source of capital.

Derivative
Transaction or contract whose value depends on that of underlying assets.

Discount
A reduction in value or the act of reducing value. In finance refers to calculating the present value of a future cash flow using a discount rate (cost of capital). Discounting is the opposite of compounding.

Dividend

A dividend is a portion of a company's earnings that is paid out to shareholders on a quarterly or annual basis.

Donation-Based Crowdfunding

Crowdfunding the relies on donations from the public, often with a promise of a sample of the product when completed. Examples include IndieGoGo and Kickstarter.

Economic Benefit Stream

This benefit stream is 'economic' because it is either derived by recasting financial statements or determined on a pro forma basis. Streams may be comprised of earnings, cash flow, and/or distributions.

Economic Life

The period of time over which property may generate economic benefits. Often the amount of time a piece of equipment is expected to last.

Economies of Scale

Efficiencies created by increasing the size of an enterprise when there are high fixed costs versus variable costs. The increased output spreads the fixed costs more thinly across the output units thereby increasing margin.

Effective Interest Rate

Interest rate after applying the "terms cost".

Efficient Market

A market in which new information is available to all parties and is very quickly reflected accurately in asset prices.

Efficient Portfolio

A portfolio that provides the greatest expected return for a given level of risk, or equivalently, the lowest risk for a given expected return.

Emerging Markets
The financial markets of developing economies.

Enterprise
See Business Enterprise.

Entity
In business it is a separate or self-contained body that provides goods or services.

Eurobond
A bond that is (1) underwritten by an international syndicate, (2) offered at issuance simultaneously to investors in a number of countries, and (3) issued outside the jurisdiction of any single country.

Eurodollar
U.S. dollars deposited in foreign banks or foreign branches of U.S. banks.

Finance
A discipline concerned with determining value and making decisions. The finance function allocates resources, which includes acquiring, investing, and managing resources.

Financial Engineer
One who combines or divides existing financial methods or instruments to create new financial products or services.

Financial Intermediaries
Brokers or arrangers of financial transactions, or institutions (such as banks) that take deposits from one party and then make loans to other parties.

Fiscal Policy
Government policy regarding taxation and spending. Fiscal policy is made by Congress and Administration.

Globalization
Tendency toward a worldwide investment environment, and the integration of national capital markets.

Gross Domestic Product (GDP)
The total value of goods and services produced in the national economy in a given year,

Idiosyncratic Risk
The portion of total risk specific to an individual security that can be avoided through diversification. See Unsystematic Risk or Company-Specific Risk

Inflation
An increase in the general price level of goods and services; alternatively, a decrease in the purchasing power of the dollar or other currency.

Information Asymmetry
A situation involving information that is known to some but not all participants.

Information Efficiency
The speed and accuracy with which prices reflect new information.

Information Opacity
Condition caused by private shareholders aversion, or inability, to grant potential capital providers with all pertinent information about their companies financial outlook, current operations and future prospects.

Intellectual Property
An original idea or concept of the creator that can be trademarked, patented, copyrighted, or held as a trade secret.

Intermediation
Assisting the exchange process in a market.

Internal Rate of Return
Discount rate at which investment has a net present value equal to zero.

LIBOR
The London Interbank Offered Rate; the rate of interest that major international banks in London charge each other for borrowings.

Liquidity
The amount and ease by which an asset can be converted to cash. Frequently measure by the current ratio.

Lockbox
A collection and processing service provided to firms by financial institutions that collect payments from a dedicated postal box that the firm directs its customers to send payment to. Located geographically to reduce mail time.

Lower Middle Market
Businesses with annual revenues between $5MM and $100MM.

Market Mechanisms
An organized set of activities that enable people to exchange or invest.

Market Penetration
The amount of revenue of a particular company as a percentage of the total theoretical size of their market.

Marketability
The ability to quickly convert property to cash at minimal cost. See Liquidity.

Migration
Movement of customers from the commercial or corporate part of the bank to the more strictly monitored asset-based lending group.

Monetary Policy
A federal government policy pursued by the Federal Reserve to control interest rates and the money supply.

Niche
A small part of a market that has potential for profitable exploitation.

Option
Gives the buyer the right, but not the obligation, to buy or sell an asset at a set price on or before a given date.

Option Price
Also called the option premium, the price paid by the buyer of the options contract for the right to buy or sell a security at a specified price in the future.

Pareto's Law
The 80/20 Rule that applies to innumerable situations. For example, 80% of profits come from 20% of the deals.

Pari Passu
Pari Passu translates as "without partiality" from Latin. It is used in reference to two classes of securities or obligations that have equal entitlement to payment.

Payback Period
The length of time it takes to recover the initial cost of a project, without regard to the time value of money.

Perquisite
Personal benefits accruing to owners or employees of a business that is derived from sources other than wages.

Portfolio
A collection of investments, real and/or financial.

Portfolio Theory
Theory holding that the risk inherent in any single asset, when held in a group of assets, is different from the inherent risk of that asset in isolation. Used to manage a collection of risky assets.

Present Value
The value today of a future payment, or stream of payments, discounted at some appropriate interest rate.

Private Capital Access Index
A quarterly index produced by Pepperdine University that measures the level to which private businesses have been able to access funding. Index values range between 0 and 100.

Private Capital Demand Index
A quarterly index produced by Pepperdine University that measures the demand for growth capital by private businesses. Index values range between 0 and 100.

Private Return Expectation
The expected rate of return that the private capital markets require in order to attract funds to a particular investment. .

Rational Expectations
The idea that people rationally anticipate the future and respond to what they see ahead.

Regulation
The attempt to bring the market under the control of an authority.

Risk
Degree of uncertainty of return on an asset. Often defined as the standard deviation of the return on total investment.

Securitization
The process of creating a passthrough, such as the mortgage pass-through security, by which the pooled assets become standard securities backed by those assets. Also, refers to the replacement of non-marketable loans and/or cash flows provided by financial intermediaries with negotiable securities issued in the public capital markets.

SIC
Abbreviated for Standard Industrial Classifications. Each 4-digit code represents a unique business activity.

Simple Interest
Interest computed on principle alone, as opposed to compound interest which includes accrued interest in the calculation.

Specific Industry Return
The average expected return for investors in companies within a certain industry.

Stakeholders
All parties that have an interest, financial or otherwise, in a firm. Includes stockholders, creditors, bondholders, employees, customers, management, the community, and the government.

Standard Deviation
A statistical measure of a probability distribution measuring the degree to which a specific value in a probability distribution varies from the expected return or value.

Structural Capital
The hardware, software, databases, organizational structure, and everything else of organizational capability that supports employee productivity.

Sunk Costs
Costs that have been incurred and cannot be reversed.

Symmetrical Information
Parties in an exchange have access to the same information.

Systematic Risk
The risk common to all securities that cannot be eliminated through diversification. When using the capital asset pricing model systematic risk is measured by beta.

Accounting Terms

Accretive
Growth by gradual addition. In finance, an action is accretive if it adds to earnings per share.

Accrual Basis
Revenues and expenses are recognized in the period in which they are incurred rather than the period that they are received or paid.

Aging Schedule
A table of accounts receivable broken down into age categories (such as 0-30 days, 30-60 days, and 60-90 days), which is used to see whether customer payments are keeping close to schedule.

AICPA
American Institute of Certified Public Accountants. The world's largest association of accountants, setting ethical standards, lobbying and providing the CPA exam.

Asset
Any item that has tangible value and can be sold or exchanged for something else that possesses value.

Asset-Light
Refers to a business that is quickly scalable because of an exceptionally high fixed asset turnover ratio. These businesses typically have a high ROIC relative to other firms in their industry.

Audited Statements
Reports in which a public accountant has verified the accuracy of transaction recording and preparation methodology.

Balance Sheet
A financial statement that shows the assets, liabilities, and owners' equity of an entity at a particular date.

Book Value
For valuation purposes, equals total assets minus intangible assets and liabilities from the balance sheet.

Break-Even Point
The point at which revenues and costs are equal; a combination of sales and costs that will yield a no profit/no loss operation.

Capital
Long-term funds invested in a firm. Consists of equity and long-term debt. Liabilities maturing in less than one year are considered working capital, not capital.

Capital Asset
A long-term asset that is not purchased or sold in the normal course of business. Generally, it includes fixed assets, e.g., land, buildings, furniture, equipment, fixtures and furniture.

Capital Efficiency
Maximizing returns while employing the least amount of capital possible. Often measured by Return on Capital Employed (ROCE).

Capital Employed
Total liabilities less non-interest bearing liabilities.

Capital Expenditure
CAPEX is the amount used during a particular period to acquire or improve long-term assets such as property, plant, or equipment.

Capital Gain or Loss
The difference between the market and book value of a capital asset at the time of transaction.

Capital Lease
A lease obligation that has to be capitalized on the balance sheet.

Cash Burn Rate
The monthly rate of cash loss in a business.

Cash Flow
Cash that is generated over a period of time by an asset, group of assets, or business enterprise.

Chart of Accounts
A list of ledger account names and associated numbers arranged in the order in which they normally appear in the financial statements.

Compound Annual Growth Rate (CAGR)
The year over year growth rate applied to an investment or other part of a company.

Correlation Coefficient
A standardized statistical measure of the dependence of two random variables, defined as the covariance divided by the standard deviations of two variables.

Cost of Goods Sold (COGS)
A figure representing the cost of buying raw materials and producing finished goods.

Current Assets
Those assets of a company that are reasonably expected to be realized in cash, or sold, or consumed during the normal operating cycle of the business (usually one year).

Current Liabilities
Liabilities that are due within the next year.

Current Maturities of Long-Term Debt
That portion of long term obligations, which is due within the next fiscal year.

Current Ratio
A measure of the liquidity of a business. Current assets divided by current liabilities.

Depreciation
A non-cash charge that reduces the accounting value of fixed assets due to wear, age or obsolescence.

Depreciation Tax Shield
The value of the tax write-off on depreciation of plant and equipment.

Dividend
A dividend is a portion of a company's earnings that is paid out to shareholders on a quarterly or annual basis.

Earnings Before Interest and Taxes (EBIT)
The figure for operating income after depreciation but without allowing for debt service or what is owed to the government for taxes.

Earnings Before Interest, Taxes, Depreciation and Amor
Earnings before interest, taxes, depreciation, and amortization.

EBITDAR
Earnings before interest, taxes, depreciation, amortization and rent.

Economic Benefit Stream
This benefit stream is 'economic' because it is either derived by recasting financial statements or determined on a pro forma basis. Streams may be comprised of earnings, cash flow, and/or distributions.

Equity Net Cash Flows
Those cash flows available to pay out to equity holders (in the form of dividends) after funding operations of the business enterprise, making necessary capital investments, and reflecting increases or decreases in debt financing. See Cash Flow to Equity.

FASB
Financial Accounting Standards Board

Financial Accounting Standards Board (FASB)
An accounting oversight committee that sets accounting standards for U.S. firms.

Fiscal Year
The declared accounting year for a company.

Fixed Asset
A long-term tangible asset that is not expected to be converted into cash in the current or upcoming fiscal year.

Fixed Asset Turnover Ratio
Ratio of net sales to fixed assets. A company that has a high fixed asset turnover ratio is considered to be "asset-light" and thus more scalable.

Fixed Charge
Current fixed obligations on a cash basis.

Fixed Charge Coverage Ratio (FCC)
A measure often used to determine probablility of default. Defined as (EBITDA. - CAPEX - Taxes) / (Interest + Principal).

Fixed Expenses
Expenses that remain the same regardless of production or sales volume in contrasts with Variable Expenses.

Free Cash Flow
Net income plus non-cash charges to income, specifically depreciation and amortization less capital expenditures, to sustain the basic business.

Free Cash Flow to Equity
Those cash flows available to pay out to equity holders (in the form of dividends) after funding operations of the business enterprise, making necessary capital investments, and reflecting increases or decreases in debt financing. See Equity Net Cash Flow.

Future Value
The amount of money that an investment made today (the present value) will grow to by some future date. Since money has time value, we naturally expect the future value to be greater than the present value. The difference between the two depends on the number of compounding periods involved and the interest rate.

General Ledger
The accounting records that show all the financial statement accounts of a business.

Generally Accepted Accounting Principles (GAAP)
A technical accounting term that encompasses the conventions, rules, and procedures necessary to define accepted accounting practice at a particular time.

Goodwill
The intangible asset arising as a result of name, reputation, customer loyalty, location, products, and similar factors not separately identified.

Goodwill Value
The value attributable to goodwill.

Gross Profit
Net sales minus cost of sales (aka Gross Margin).

Gross Sales
The total revenue at invoice value prior to any discounts or allowances,

Impaired Goodwill
According to SFAS 142, if goodwill carried on the balance sheet is worth more than its current "fair value," the difference must be written off.

Impairment Test
Test for goodwill impairment at the reporting unit level.

Income Statement
The financial statement that summarizes the revenues and expenses of a company over a specified period of time.

Intangible Assets
Non-physical assets (such as franchises, trademarks, patents, copyrights, goodwill, equities, mineral rights, securities, and contracts as distinguished from physical assets) that grant rights, privileges, and have economic benefits for the owner.

Intellectual Assets
Intangible assets particular to a company that add to the enterprise value.

Interest
The price paid for the borrowing money

Interest Expense
The cost of borrowing funds in the current period.

Leverage
The use of debt to improve the financial performance of an enterprise. Can also specifically refer to an accounting ratio that measure the proportion of debt in the capital structure of a company, such as the debt/equity ratio.

Long-Term Liabilities
Liabilities of a business due in more than one year. An example of a long-term liability would be mortgage payable.

MACRS
Modified accelerated cost recovery system.

Margin Appreciation
An increase in the gross margin of a company.

Mean
The expected value of a random variable.

Median
The value of the midpoint variable when the data are arranged in ascending or descending order.

Minority Interest
An ownership interest less than fifty percent (50%) of the voting interest in a business enterprise

Net Asset Value
The adjustment of a company's assets and liabilities to market values.

Non-Cash Charge
A cost, such as depreciation, depletion, or amortization, that does not involve any cash outflow.

Non-Operating Assets
Assets not necessary to ongoing operations of the business enterprise.

Normalized Capital Expenditures
Expected average capital expenditures.

Operating Expense
The amount paid for asset maintenance or the cost of doing business.

Operating Income
Revenue less cost of goods sold less operating expenses.

Operating Lease
Lease extended for small part of the useful life of the equipment. Lessor expected to return the equipment after term.

Operating Profit
Gross Profit minus Operating Expenses.

Price/Earnings Ratio
Shows the "multiple" of earnings at which a public stock sells.

Pro Forma Earnings
Projected earnings.

Pro Forma Statement
A financial statement showing the forecast or projected operating results and balance sheet, as in pro forma income statements, balance sheets, and statements of cash flows.

Recast EBIT
Recast earnings before interest and taxes.

Recast EBITDA
Recast earnings before interest, taxes, depreciation, and amortization.

Reporting Unit
In impaired goodwill, an operating division for which management has reviewed and assessed performance.

Retained Earnings
Profits of the business that have not been paid out to the owners as of the balance sheet date.

Return on Capital Employed (ROCE)
A common measure of Capital Efficiency. Defined as EBIT / (Total Assets - Current Liabilities).

Return on Equity (ROE)
Measure of the overall efficiency of the firm in managing its total investments in assets and in generating a return to stockholders.

Return on Invested Capital (ROIC)
A measure of a company's capital efficiency. Defined as (net income - dividends) / (long-term debt + current portion of long-term debt + shareholders equity + capitalized lease obligations - cash - net assets of discontinued operations).

ROA
Return on assets.

Shareholders' Equity
A company's total assets minus total liabilities, or a company's net worth.

Standard Deviation
A statistical measure of a probability distribution measuring the degree to which a specific value in a probability distribution varies from the expected return or value.

Tangible asset
An asset whose value depends on particular physical properties.

Treasury Stock
Common stock that has been repurchased by the company and held in the company's treasury.

Working Capital
Current assets minus current liabilities (excluding short-term debt).

Write-down
Decreasing the book value of an asset if its book value is overstated compared to current market values.

Investment Banking Terms

Best-Efforts Sale
The underwriting firm agrees to sell as much of the offering as possible and return any unsold shares to the issuer.

Call for Offers
Made by the intermediary of a private auction after buyer visits to gain a better perspective of the potential suitors.

Flotation Costs
The total costs of issuing and selling a public security.

Investment Banker
Financial intermediary who assists companies in accessing the capital markets and performs a variety of services, including aiding in the sale of securities, facilitating mergers and other corporate reorganizations.

Lehman Formula
A compensation formula originally developed by investment bankers Lehman Brothers for investment banking services: 5% of the first million dollars involved in the transaction for services needed, 4% of the second million, 3% of the third million, 2% of the fourth million, 1% of everything thereafter.

No Shop
Period stipulated in a letter of intent within which the company or its agents cannot solicit other investor interest.

Offering Memorandum
A document that outlines the terms of securities to be offered in a private placement.

One-Step Auction
Auction that concurrently encourages interest within a limited group of buyers.

Private Investment Banker
One that helps private companies access the private capital markets.

Red Herring
A preliminary registration statement describing the issue (the IPO) and prospects of the company that must be filed with the SEC or provincial securities commission.

Selling Memorandum
Document that disseminates information to potential buyers during an auction.

Shell Company
Existing public company in a reverse merger.

Two-Step Auction
Each step of the selling process is staged using deadlines.

Underwriter
Securities firm that purchases securities from the issuer and then sells them in an underwritten public offering.

Private Equity Terms

2/20 Fee Model
An investment fund where investors pay a 2% management fee plus 20% carried interest (aka incentive fee).

Accelerator
An accelerator is similar to an incubator, in that accelerators provide infrastructure and mentoring, but they are typically profit-driven. Participants have a limited time in the incubator (often 3 months) with the goal of Series A funding at the end. The accelerator generally takes some equity in each startup.

Accretive
Growth by gradual addition. In finance, an action is accretive if it adds to earnings per share.

Add-On Acquisition
A horizontal purchase of similar company that increases the size of or compliments the platform company.

Alternative Investment
Investments other than cash or publicly traded stocks and bonds. Generally illiquid and require the investor to be an accredited investor. Can include real estate (and other real assets), hedge funds, angel investments, venture capital, private equity, and private debt.

Asset-Light
Refers to a business that is quickly scalable because of an exceptionally high fixed asset turnover ratio. These businesses typically have a high ROIC relative to other firms in their industry.

BIMBO
Buy/In Management Buyout. Transaction in which business is bought out by a management team comprised of existing and incoming management.

BIO
Institutional buyout where an equity sponsor introduces new management.

Boilerplate
Standard terms and conditions. Don't accept these at face value. Hire a securities attorney to review.

Bolt-On Acquisition
A horizontal acquisition that is done primarily to increase the size (revenue) of the platform company.

Burn-Out Round
This is a venture capital funding round for a company that is not doing well, so the share price is very low (a down round) which means that the new infusion of capital results in a high level of dilution of the stakes of the investors in prior rounds. Also known as wash-out round or a cram-down round.

Business Development Company (BDC)
A Venture Capital firm that is publicly traded, thus allowing retail investors to invest in this asset class.

Capital Efficiency
Maximizing returns while employing the least amount of capital possible. Often measured by Return on Capital Employed (ROCE).

Carried Interest
A percentage of an investment fund's capital gains that is paid to the fund's general partner. See incentive fee.

Catch-Up
An alternative investment fund fee structure where there is an overall incentive fee even when there is a hurdle rate in place. Thus, as soon as the hurdle rate is satisfied, the fund enters a "catch-up" phase, where all additional gains to go the general partner until the point is reached where the overall incentive fee percentage has been paid. After that, gains are split between the general partner and limited partners according to the normal schedule.

Clawback
A provision in an alternative investment fund fee structure where the general partner must refund a portion of incentive fees paid on early harvesting activities if later lower fund performance doesn't justify those incentive fees overall.

Co-Investment
An opportunity offered to a limited partner to make a direct investment (outside of the fund) to a fund's portfolio company.

Committed Capital
The amount that has been pledged to an investment fund by investors, but not yet paid to the fund.

Control Buyout
A purchase of equity that results in the acquirer getting a controlling majority of the company's shares.

Conversion Rights
Provisions set forth in the term sheet regarding the preferred stock conversion ratio and whether or not the ratio is fluctuating.

Convertible Debt
A debt instrument that can be exercised into the equity security of the debtor in accordance with the conditions set forth in the debt instrument.

Convertible Preferred Stock
Preferred stock that can be converted into common stock at the option of the holder.

Cram-Down Round
This is a venture capital funding round for a company that is not doing well, so the share price is very low (a down round) which means that the new infusion of capital results in a high level of dilution of the stakes of the investors in prior rounds. Also known as burn-out round or a wash-out round.

Crowdfunding
Raising money online in small amounts from many people (often unsophisticated). There are three categories of crowdfunding: Donation-Based Crowdfunding, Debt-Based Crowdfunding, and Equity-Based Crowdfunding.

Deal Sourcing
The process of finding acquisition target candidates in M&A and private equity.

Deleveraging Transaction
Any transaction that reduces a firm's debt. Commonly refers to conversion of convertible debt into stock.

Dilutive
In finance, an action is dilutive if it results in decreased earnings per share.

Down Round
A series of venture funding where the share price is lower than the previous round of funding. This is bad for previous investors because it is highly dilutive.

Drag Along Rights
Entitlement of the majority stakeholder to force a minority stakeholder to join a transaction where it is selling its stake.

Dry Powder
Metaphorically refers to dry gunpowder, meaning that the possessor of dry powder has the ability to continue to fight. In finance, this means that the investor still has a cash reserve with which to make additional investments.

Dutch Auction
An auction where the bidding starts at a high price and then the auctioneer incrementally lowers the price until it reaches a point where the entire offering is sold.

Early Stage
An enterprise that have been operational less than three years, may have revenue, unlikely to be profitable.

Earn-Out
Method for triggering changes in the purchase price based on future performance of the subject company. The seller "earns" a portion of the purchase price by the company meeting ageed-upon future performance milestones.

Enterprise Value
Value of 100% of the ownership.

Equity Penalties
Agreements that increase an investor's percentage of ownership upon the occurrence of a certain event.

Equity Recapitalization
A private equity technique where the company sells a portion of the company to a PEG (using a mix of debt and equity) allowing the founder to have a partial liquidity event. The founder retains some ownership and stays involved for a number of additional years until a full buyout occurs, giving the founder a second bite at the apple.

Equity Split
Percentage of the company that each investor owns.

Equity Sponsor
Private equity provider that finances a buyout for a management team.

Equity Sponsored Buyout
A management team partners with an equity sponsor (provider) to perform a buyout.

Equity Upside
When a capital provider experiences a gain when the company succeeds.

Equity-Based Crowdfunding
Crowdfunding where investors get equity shares of the startups. Under Regulation A+ even non-accredited investors can invest.

Exit
An event for a private business that allows equity investors to sell their shares, such as an LBO or an acquisition.

Exit Strategy
Investor insistence on certain rights so they may realize the value of their investment if they see fit to exit.

Expansion Stage
An enterprise that in experiencing rapid growth, may or may not be profitable.

Financial Barn Raising
The act of soliciting a placement by leveraging community relationships.

Financial Control Premium
Control value of an enterprise based on financial returns.

Financial Sponsor
The financial sponsor in a deal is typically the private equity firm that manages a leveraged buyout.

Fund Lifetime
An investment fund typically has a finite life, which is often ten years (plus two optional one-year extensions at the discretion of the general partner).

Fundless Sponsor
A private equity investor that invests their own funds directly rather than as a limited partner in an investment fund. (a.k.a Independent Sponsor).

Fundraising
The early phase of an alternative investment fund where the general partner seeks limited partner investors to committed capital. The manager of the fund typical contributes up to 5% of the raise.

General Partner
In an FLP, usually the parents or corporation owned by the parents typically holding a nominal partnership interest.

Going Private
Publicly owned stock is replaced with complete equity ownership by a private group.

Going Public
Undergoing an initial public offering.

Hard Hurdle
Incentive fee doesn't start until after fund reaches hurdle rate. With catch-up, all profits go to incentive fee after hurdle rate is achieved, until overall carried interest rate to manager has been reached.

Harvest Period
In private equity, this is typically the last five years of the fund, when portfolio companies are sold.

Horizontal Integration
Merger or acquisition involving two or more firms in the same
industry in the same position in the supply chain.

Hurdle Rate
The minimum return that a fund must reach before incentive fees
are paid.

Incentive Fee
A percentage of an investment fund's capital gains that is paid to
the fund's general partner. See carried interest.

Incubator
An organization that provides infrastructure and mentoring for
startups. They are often sponsored by local governments.

Independent Sponsor
A private equity investor that invests their own funds directly
rather than as a limited partner in an investment fund. (a.k.a
Fundless Sponsor).

Inflection Point
A significant change in the progress or direction of a company.

Invested Capital
The amount of an investment fund's committed capital that has
actually been invested by the general partner.

Investee
Entity that receives capital.

Investment Horizon
Timeframe within which an investor will exit an investment.

Investment Period
Generally the first three to five years of a private equity or venture
capital fund, when the general partner finds companies to invest in.

Investment Round
A single attempt to raise capital through the issuance of stock.

Investor's Rights
Privileges of the investor outlined in the term sheet.

Later Stage
Venture capital funding rounds that are after startup / Series A, meaning Series B and beyond.

Lehman Formula
A compensation formula originally developed by investment bankers Lehman Brothers for investment banking services: 5% of the first million dollars involved in the transaction for services needed, 4% of the second million, 3% of the third million, 2% of the fourth million, 1% of everything thereafter.

Leverage
The use of debt to improve the financial performance of an enterprise. Can also specifically refer to an accounting ratio that measure the proportion of debt in the capital structure of a company, such as the debt/equity ratio.

Leveraged Buyout (LBO)
The use of borrowed money to finance the purchase of a firm.

Leveraged Recapitalization
When a company takes on significant debt in order to pay dividends or repurchase stock. See Equity Recapitalization.

Limited Partner
A partner who has limited legal liability for the obligations of the partnership.

Liquidation Preference
In the event of an IPO or acquisition, this indicates the order in which investors get paid and how much. 1x liquidation preference means the investor gets 100% of original investment back before the remaining capital gains are split among all investors.

Majority Interest
An ownership interest greater than fifty percent (50%) of the voting interest in a business enterprise.

Margin Appreciation
An increase in the gross margin of a company.

Middle Market
A segment of privately and publicly held companies whose annual sales range from $5 million to $1 billion.

Milestones
Included in the term sheet, they set forth certain benchmarks for the company, with corresponding staged investments.

Mini-IPO
A company that raises money under Reg A+ of Title IV of the JOBS Act. Compliance and disclosure requirements are lighter than with traditional public companies.

Niche
A small part of a market that has potential for profitable exploitation.

No Shop
Period stipulated in a letter of intent within which the company or its agents cannot solicit other investor interest.

Offering Memorandum
A document that outlines the terms of securities to be offered in a private placement.

Offeror
See Issuer

Operating Partner
A member of the management team of a private equity fund who works directly with the portfolio companies to increase value.

Oversubscribed
When during the fundraising phase of an investment fund, the fundraising goal is exceeded.

Piggy Back Registration
When an underwriter allows existing holdings of shares in a corporation to be sold in conjunction with an offering of new shares.

Pipeline
The list of potential deals that are in development but typically not yet engaged.

Platform Company
Company that forms the foundation of a business. Additional companies are acquired and added to the platform.

Portfolio Company
A company owned by a private equity fund as part of their investment portfolio.

Post-Money Valuation
The "pre-money" valuation of the company plus the amount of the investment.

Preferred Return
The return that an investment fund must achieve before carried interest is paid to the general partner. A common level for the preferred return is around 8%. See Hurdle Rate.

Pre-Money Valuation
Value of a company prior to accepting further investment.

Private Equity
Refers to the various organizations that provide equity capital to private companies.

Private Equity Group (PEG)
Typically refers to the managers of a fund that invests in the equity of private companies, especially later stage firms.

Private Placement Memorandum (PPM)
Document that sets forth critical information about an offering for potential private investors.

Private Return Expectation
The expected rate of return that the private capital markets require in order to attract funds to a particular investment. .

Ratchets
Device to encourage management to perform against defined targets. Can also refer to mechanisms that prevent dilution of equity positions of current investors by future investors.

Realized Returns
The actual returns to investors from a given investment.

Registration Rights
Rights that govern the how a company goes public, who pays the cost associated with the process, and how many times it can file an IPO.

Regulation A
The securities regulation that exempts small public offerings, those valued at less than $5 million, from most registration requirements with the SEC.

Regulation A+
An SEC regulation that allows companies to raise up to $50MM from both accredited and non-accredited investors. Companies that do this are called a Mini-IPO.

Regulation D
A series of six rules, Rules 501-506, establishing transactional exemptions from the registration requirements of the 1933 Act.

Right of First Refusal
As a buy/sell provision, this right states an owner must offer to sell his shares to other owners before offering them to outsiders.

Roll-Up
Simultaneous consolidation and initial public offering.

Safe Harbor Rule
SEC Rule 147, which allows companies to raise money without registering as a public company as long as they are incorporated, do business, and solicit investors all within a single US state.

Seed Stage
Funding during the idea stage of a company. This funding generally comes from the founder, angels, or family and friends.

Series A
Typically this first round of venture capital funding for a firm. Follows angel or seed stage.

Skin-In-The-Game
In private equity, refers to the general partner of a fund investing its own money in the fund as a limited partner. This shows alignment with the interests of the investors.

Sponsored Transaction
A private capital market deal that has a financial sponsor in the lead position.

Stages of Investment
These stages enable equity providers to match the appropriate funding source with the capital need, creating efficiency in the capital allocation process. The stages are: seed stage, start-up stage, early stage, expansion stage, and later stage.

Startup Stage
The new venture is operational, but may not yet have revenue.

Syndication
The co-investment of different capital providers in a single company.

Tag Along Rights
Entitlement of minority stakeholder to join a transaction if the majority chooses to sell its stake.

Term Sheet
Document that outlines the tenets of a deal and serves as the basis for its legal drafting.

Triggering Events
Events that activate a buy/sell agreement.

Undersubscribed
At the end of the fundraising phase of an investment fund, the fundraising goal is has not been achieved.

Upper Middle Market
Businesses with annual revenues between $500MM and $1B.

Venture Capital
Money provided by professionals who invest alongside management in early to expansion stage companies that have potential to develop rapidly.

Vertical Integration
Merger in which one firm acquires another firm that is in the same industry but at another position in the supply chain.

Voting Rights
The rights to vote on matters that are put to a vote of security holders.

Wash-Out Round
This is a venture capital funding round for a company that is not doing well, so the share price is very low (a down round) which means that the new infusion of capital results in a high level of dilution of the stakes of the investors in prior rounds. Also known as burn-out round or a cram-down round.

Waterfall
The order in which gains flow to the various stakeholders in an investment fund.

Weighted Average Antidilution
Form of antidilution protection that prevents the value of shareholdings from being reduced by later share sales at lower prices.

Equity Terms

Accredited Investor
Investors who are considered by the SEC to be wealthy enough to afford to lose their investment in a worse case scenario. A single person is an accredited investor if he/she has $200,000 in annual income or a net worth of more than $1 million (excluding residence).

Acquiree
The firm being purchased in an acquisition. See Target.

Acquirer
A firm or individual that is purchasing an equity interest in another company.

Add-On Acquisition
A horizontal purchase of similar company that increases the size of or compliments the platform company.

Adjustable Rate
Preferred stock whose dividends are reset quarterly at a predetermined spread. Can also refer to a loan with an interest rate that floats at a pre-determined margin or spread above a stated index (such as LIBOR).

Adjusted Equity
Difference between the market value of a company's assets and liabilities.

All-in Cost
Total costs of a specific capital type, explicit (such as required return) and implicit (fees and other charges).

Angel Investor
Wealthy investor that participates in high-risk deals with early stage companies.

EEF (QR) - Equity Terms

Anti-Dilution Rights
Protects an investor's shares in a company from being diluted if the company issues more stock.

Armenian Handshake
Buy/Sell provision to protect minority owners. An owner cannot accept compensation from the company without sharing or getting consent from the other owners.

Beta
A measure of systematic risk of a security; the tendency of a security's returns to correlate with swings in the broad market.

Black-Scholes
A model for pricing call options that uses the stock price, the exercise price, the risk-free interest rate, the time to expiration, and the standard deviation of the historical return of the underlying stock.

Call Option
An option contract that gives its holder the right (but not the obligation) to purchase a specified number of shares of the underlying stock at the given strike price, on or before the expiration date of the contract.

Capital
Long-term funds invested in a firm. Consists of equity and long-term debt. Liabilities maturing in less than one year are considered working capital, not capital.

Capital Structure
The mix of debt and equity financing in a business.

Class of Shares
Shares of varying rights or powers that are issued by the same company (ex. Class A, Class B).

Common Stock
The most frequently issued class of stock; usually it provides a voting right but is secondary to preferred stock in dividend and liquidation rights.

Control
The power to direct the management and policies of a business enterprise.

Control Buyout
A purchase of equity that results in the acquirer getting a controlling majority of the company's shares.

Control Premium
An amount by which the pro rata value of a controlling interest exceeds the pro rata value of a noncontrolling interest in a business enterprise that reflects the power of control.

Control Value
Ownership interest of 51%-100% in the company.

Conversion Rights
Provisions set forth in the term sheet regarding the preferred stock conversion ratio and whether or not the ratio is fluctuating.

Convertible Debt
A debt instrument that can be exercised into the equity security of the debtor in accordance with the conditions set forth in the debt instrument.

Convertible Preferred Stock
Preferred stock that can be converted into common stock at the option of the holder.

Cost of Equity
The expected rate of return that an Individual investor requires in order to attract funds to a particular investment.

Cross-Purchase Agreements
Buy/Sell agreement in which one or more other parties buys a business interest from an exiting party.

Cumulative Preferred Stock
Preferred stock whose dividends accrue, should the issuer not make timely dividend payments.

Debt to Equity
Measures the risk of the firm's capital structure in terms of amounts of capital contributed by creditors and that contributed by owners.

Deleveraging Transaction
Any transaction that reduces a firm's debt. Commonly refers to conversion of convertible debt into stock.

Detachable Warrant
Warrant that may be sold separately from the security with which it was originally issued.

Dilution
In asset based lending, percentage of the total invoices uncollected. Regarding equity, a watering down in the ownership stake, usually as a result of the sale of additional shares.

Equity Kicker
Stock options or warrants to purchase stock given by a company to a lender or other party as an inducement to lend money or provide some other value.

Equity Mezzanine Capital
Subordinated debt that relies on coupon plus warrants for its return.

Equity Net Cash Flows
Those cash flows available to pay out to equity holders (in the form of dividends) after funding operations of the business enterprise, making necessary capital investments, and reflecting increases or decreases in debt financing. See Cash Flow to Equity.

Equity Penalties
Agreements that increase an investor's percentage of ownership upon the occurrence of a certain event.

Equity Recapitalization
A private equity technique where the company sells a portion of the company to a PEG (using a mix of debt and equity) allowing the founder to have a partial liquidity event. The founder retains some ownership and stays involved for a number of additional years until a full buyout occurs, giving the founder a second bite at the apple.

Equity Split
Percentage of the company that each investor owns.

Equity-Based Crowdfunding
Crowdfunding where investors get equity shares of the startups. Under Regulation A+ even non-accredited investors can invest.

Exchangeable
Preferred stock that can be exchanged into a debt security, normally at the election of the issuer.

Exercise
To implement the right of the holder of an option to buy or sell the underlying security.

Exercise Date
Date upon which the option or warrant can be purchased or sold.

Exercise Price
Price at which the stock underlying a call or put option can be purchased (call) or sold (put) over the specified period. Also called strike price.

Exit
An event for a private business that allows equity investors to sell their shares, such as an LBO or an acquisition.

Expiration
The date and time after which the option may no longer be exercised.

Expression of Interest
Document signed by the top prospects in an auction that narrows attention to the best suitors.

Features
Characteristics of a particular security such as whether or not it is convertible, redeemable, exchangeable, etc.

Flotation Costs
The total costs of issuing and selling a public security.

Free Cash Flow to Equity
Those cash flows available to pay out to equity holders (in the form of dividends) after funding operations of the business enterprise, making necessary capital investments, and reflecting increases or decreases in debt financing. See Equity Net Cash Flow.

Grant
When shares of stock are given outright, rather than just an option to buy stock at a certain price.

Growth Capital
External capital inflow to the firm that is intended for expansion of the business, rather than for working capital or refinancing purposes.

Initial Public Offering (IPO)
A company's first sale of stock to the public.

Installment Sale
The sale of an asset in exchange for a specified series of payments (the installments).

Institutional Investor
An entity, company, mutual fund, insurance corporation, brokerage, or other such group that invests.

Invested Capital
The sum of equity and debt in a business enterprise.

Investee
Entity that receives capital.

Investment Round
A single attempt to raise capital through the issuance of stock.

Issue
In securities, issue is stock or bonds sold by a corporation or a government; or, the selling of new securities by a corporation or government through an underwriter or private placement.

Issuer
Company offering securities.

Letter Stock
Privately placed common stock, so-called because the SEC requires a letter from the purchaser stating that the stock is not intended for resale.

Leverage
The use of debt to improve the financial performance of an enterprise. Can also specifically refer to an accounting ratio that measure the proportion of debt in the capital structure of a company, such as the debt/equity ratio.

Leveraged Recapitalization
When a company takes on significant debt in order to pay
dividends or repurchase stock. See Equity Recapitalization.

Majority Interest
An ownership interest greater than fifty percent (50%) of the
voting interest in a business enterprise.

Market Capitalization
The total dollar value of all outstanding shares. Computed as
shares times current market price. It is a measure of corporate size.

Marketable Minority Interest
Minority interest assumed to be freely tradable in the marketplace.

Middle Market
A segment of privately and publicly held companies whose annual
sales range from $5 million to $1 billion.

Minority Discount
A discount for lack of control applicable to a minority interest.

Minority Interest
An ownership interest less than fifty percent (50%) of the voting
interest in a business enterprise

Nonmarketable Minority Interest
Minority interest for which there is no active market.

Nonvoting Shares
Common shares with no voting rights.

Oppression
Legal term meaning the minority shareholder's reasonable
expectations have not been met.

Optimal Capital Structure
The capital structure at which firm value is maximized.

Outstanding Shares
The number of shares currently owned by all investors.

Over-the-Counter (OTC)
A computerized network (NASDAQ) through which trades of bonds, non-listed stocks, and other securities take place.

Ownership Agreements
Legal agreements that define the rights and privileges of the owners.

Participating Preferred
Convertible preferred stock that provides the holder with extraordinary rights in the event the company is sold or liquidated.

Penny Warrants
Warrant that has a nominal price to the investor.

Performance Ratchets
Incentive bonuses written into finance agreements that encourages management to perform.

Phantom Stock
Right to a bonus based upon the performance of shares of a corporation's common stock (without actually receiving those shares) over a specified period of time.

Piggy Back Registration
When an underwriter allows existing holdings of shares in a corporation to be sold in conjunction with an offering of new shares.

Pink Sheets
Listings of price quotes for companies that trade in the over the counter market.

Poof IPO
See Roll-Up

Preemptive Rights
The rights of the investor to acquire new securities issued by the company to the extent necessary to maintain its percentage interest on a converted basis.

Preferences
Advantages granted to owners of preferred stock (versus common stock)

Preferred Stock
A security that shows ownership in a corporation and gives the holder a claim, prior to the claim of common stockholders, on earnings and also generally on assets in the event of liquidation. Preferred stock of public companies generally does not have voting rights, whereas preferred stock in private companies often has super-voting rights.

Pre-IPO Studies
Conducted to determine a stock's marketability discount upon initial offering.

Private Annuities
Transfer of stock in exchange for an unsecured promise to receive a stream of fixed payments for the life of the seller.

Private Auction
Selling process in which an intermediary simultaneously contacts a limited number of prospects in an attempt to confidentially maximize the selling price.

Private Capital Markets
Markets where private debt and equity are raised and exchanged.

Private Corporation
A corporation that ownership is held by the private sector, i.e. individuals or companies,

Private Equity
Refers to the various organizations that provide equity capital to private companies.

Private Equity Group (PEG)
Typically refers to the managers of a fund that invests in the equity of private companies, especially later stage firms.

Private Investment Banker
One that helps private companies access the private capital markets.

Private Placement
A nonpublic offering of securities exempt from full SEC registration made directly by the issuing company, but can also be made by an underwriter.

Proportionate Interests
Notion that dissenting shareholders have the right to see their equity stake valued on a going concern basis rather than a liquidation basis.

Public Markets
Markets where public debt and equity are raised and exchanged.

Put Option
The right but not the obligation to sell an underlying at a particular price (strike price) on or before the expiration date of the contract.

Redeemable
Preferred stock that can be redeemed by the issuer at a specified price.

Restricted Stock Studies
Examine the issuance of restricted common stock of companies with actively traded public shares.

Return on Equity (ROE)
Measure of the overall efficiency of the firm in managing its total investments in assets and in generating a return to stockholders.

Reverse Merger
A private company goes public by purchasing a public company shell, then using that shell to acquire the original private company.

Right of First Refusal
As a buy/sell provision, this right states an owner must offer to sell his shares to other owners before offering them to outsiders.

Rule 504
A business using this Reg. D offering can raise a maximum of $1 million less the total dollar amount of securities sold during the preceding twelve month period under Rule 504.

Rule 505
This Reg. D offering may not exceed $5 million less the total dollar amount of securities sold during the preceding twelve month period under Rule 504, Rule 505 or Section 3(b) of the Act.

Rule 506
This Reg. D offering provides an exemption for limited offers and sales without regard to the dollar amount of the offering.

SCOR
Small Corporate Offering Registration. An "IPO-Lite" available under Reg A with reduced documentation and disclosures.

Secondary Market
The exchange or over-the-counter market where shares are traded after the initial offering.

Series A
Typically this first round of venture capital funding for a firm. Follows angel or seed stage.

Shared Control Value
Level where no block of ownership has more than 50% of the shares.

Shareholder Agreement
Agreement that sets the terms by which shareholders deal with each other.

Shareholders' Equity
A company's total assets minus total liabilities, or a company's net worth.

Shares
Certificates or book entries representing ownership in a corporation or similar entity.

Shell Company
Existing public company in a reverse merger.

Should-Be-Private Company
Company whose costs of being public outweigh its benefits.

Spin-Off
When a large enterprise takes one of its divisions and makes it a stand-alone company.

Stock Appreciation Rights
Rights granted to employees to receive a benefit equal to the appreciation of a given number of shares over a specified period.

Stock Exchanges
Formal organizations, approved and regulated by the Securities & Exchange Commission (SEC), that are made up of members that use the facilities to exchange certain common stocks.

Stock Market
Also called the equity market, the market for trading equities.

Stock Option
Right to buy a certain number of shares in the company at a fixed price for a certain number of years. See Call Option.

Stockholder
Holder of equity shares in a firm.

Strike Price
The stated price per share for which underlying stock may be purchased (in the case of a call) or sold (in the case of a put) by the option holder upon exercise of the option contract.

Supermajority
Provision in a company's charter requiring a majority of, say, 80% of shareholders to approve certain changes, such as a merger.

Synergistic Buyer
The strategic acquirer in a synergistic relationship. See Strategic Buyer.

Treasury Stock
Common stock that has been repurchased by the company and held in the company's treasury.

Venture Capital
Money provided by professionals who invest alongside management in early to expansion stage companies that have potential to develop rapidly.

Voting Rights
The rights to vote on matters that are put to a vote of security holders.

Warrant
A security entitling the holder to buy a proportionate amount of stock at some specified future date at a specified price, usually one higher than current market.

Weighted Average Antidilution
Form of antidilution protection that prevents the value of shareholdings from being reduced by later share sales at lower prices.

Debt Financing Terms

7(a) Loan Guaranty Program
SBA program that provides loan guarantees to small businesses unable to secure financing on reasonable terms through normal lending channels. Maximum loan is $5 million and loan term is 25 years for real estate, 10 years for equipment and 7 years for working capital. 7(a) loans are fully amortized.

Acceleration Clause
A legal clause stating that the entire outstanding balance of a loan becomes payable immediately if a certain event occurs.

Affirmative Covenant
A covenant that requires the borrower to take a particular action. The borrower will be in breach unless that action is taken.

All-in Cost
Total costs of a specific capital type, explicit (such as required return) and implicit (fees and other charges).

Amortization
The process of spreading the cost of an intangible asset over the expected useful life of the asset, or the repayment of the principal of a loan by installments.

Audit Fee
Fee charged by a lender for monitoring the borrower's collateral position and financial statements.

Balance Sheet Leverage Ratio
A standard measure of company leverage. Defined as Debt divided by Equity.

Balloon Payment
The balance, or final payment after monthly payments of principal and interest are paid on a loan.

Bank Lessors
When a bank provides the equipment lease, rather than a finance company or the equipment vendor.

Bankruptcy
State of being insolvent and thus unable to pay debts.

Basel III
An international regulatory scheme for banks related to stress testing, capitalization, and liquidity risk.

Basis Point
One hundredth of a percentage point.

Bond
A debt instrument which pays back cash to the holder at regular frequencies. The payment is normally a fixed percentage, known as a coupon. At maturity, the face value of the bond is paid.

Borrowing Base
The amount that can be borrowed at a given time. Found by applying advance rates against eligible assets.

Borrowing Base Certificate
Report prepared by a borrower that shows the amount that can be borrowed at a given time.

Bridge Financing
Interim financing (often high interest debt) of one sort or another used to solidify a position until more permanent financing is arranged.

Business & Industry Loans
Loans provided to rural companies with stipulation that a job must be created or retained for each $40,000 loaned.

Business Bank
A financial institution that provides business loans generally between $1MM and $3MM.

Call Protection
This is a prepayment penalty that prevents the lender from losing profit on a loan if the borrower repays early.

Cap
An upper limit on the interest rate on a floating-rate note.

Capital Employed
Total liabilities less non-interest bearing liabilities.

Capital Lease
A lease obligation that has to be capitalized on the balance sheet.

Capital Structure
The mix of debt and equity financing in a business.

Capitalization Rate
Any divisor used to convert a benefit stream into value.

CAPLine Program
Umbrella program under which the SBA helps small businesses meet their short-term and cyclical working capital needs.

Captive Lessors
Subsidiaries of manufacturers that provide financing to customers in the form of an equipment lease.

Cash Flow Leverage Ratio
A measure often used to determine probablility of default. Defined as (Debt / EBITDA).

Cash Flow Loan
A loan where repayment probability is measured based on the cash flow of the borrower.

Certified Development Company 504 Program
SBA program that provides growing businesses with long-term fixed-rate financing for major fixed assets, such as land and buildings.

Chapter 11
Voluntary bankruptcy filing by the debtor.

Chapter 7
Involuntary liquidation forced by creditor(s).

Closing Fee
A fee charged by the lender at closing to cover such items as the funding fee, processing fees, underwriter's fee, etc.

Collateral
Assets that secure a loan or other debt.

Collateral Monitoring
Process of ensuring that the assets that the borrower provided as collateral are maintained.

Collateral Value
The value of a business interest for secured lending purposes.

Commercial Bank
A financial institution that provides business loans between $3MM and $50MM.

Commitment Fee
A fee paid to a commercial bank in return for its legal commitment to lend funds that have not yet been advanced. It the loan happens, it becomes the origination fee.

Community Bank
A financial institution that provides business loans generally less than $1MM.

Compensating Balance
An excess balance that is left in a bank to provide indirect compensation for loans extended or services provided.

Compound Interest
Interest calculated from the total of original principal plus accrued interest.

Contingent Liability
A liability that is dependent upon uncertain events that may occur in the future.

Convertible Debt
A debt instrument that can be exercised into the equity security of the debtor in accordance with the conditions set forth in the debt instrument.

Corporate Bank
A financial institution that provides business loans generally more than $50MM.

Coupon
Interest payment on debt.

Covenants
Rules attached to a loan agreement that govern what the borrower can and cannot do during the loan term. Maintaining certain financial statement ratios is common.

Credit Box
The qualification boundaries that must be met in order to qualify for a particular source of capital.

Credit Scoring
An analytical process designed to predict whether loan application would live up to their debt obligations.

Creditor
Lender of money.

Cure Period
A period of time specified in the loan agreement within which the borrower has to mend any violations of the loan covenant.

Debt Capacity
Ability to borrow. The amount a firm can borrow up to the point where the firm value no longer increases.

Debt Service
Interest payment plus repayments of principal to creditors, that is, retirement of debt.

Debt to Equity
Measures the risk of the firm's capital structure in terms of amounts of capital contributed by creditors and that contributed by owners.

Debt-Based Crowdfunding
Crowdfunding where the public lends the borrower small amounts of money, adding up to the amount desired. Also called social lending or peer-to-peer lending. Examples are Prosper.com and LendingClub.

Debtor
1) In lending, it is the borrower. 2) In factoring, it is the entity that generates the receivable.

Default
The failure to make a payment on either the interest or principle of a debt or loan.

Default Interest Rates
Percentage increase over that of the agreed upon interest rate for violations of the loan agreement.

Default Risk
The risk that a company will be unable to pay the principal or contractual interest on its debt obligations.

Deferred Interest Balloon
Structure that defers a stated amount of interest into the future, at which point it is due in full.

Deleveraging Transaction
Any transaction that reduces a firm's debt. Commonly refers to conversion of convertible debt into stock.

Demand Loan Payment
The lender can call (cancel and demand full repayment) at any time.

Dodd-Frank
Refers to The Dodd-Frank Wall Street Reform and Consumer Protection Act, passed in 2010. Implemented additional monitoring for financial institutions deemed "too big to fail" and imposed additional restrictions on lending to consumers. Also imposed the Volcker Rule to limit speculative trading by banks.

Equity Kicker
Stock options or warrants to purchase stock given by a company to a lender or other party as an inducement to lend money or provide some other value.

Equity Mezzanine Capital
Subordinated debt that relies on coupon plus warrants for its return.

Equity Recapitalization
A private equity technique where the company sells a portion of the company to a PEG (using a mix of debt and equity) allowing the founder to have a partial liquidity event. The founder retains some ownership and stays involved for a number of additional years until a full buyout occurs, giving the founder a second bite at the apple.

Equity Upside
When a capital provider experiences a gain when the company succeeds.

Exchangeable
Preferred stock that can be exchanged into a debt security, normally at the election of the issuer.

Export Working Capital Program
SBA program designed to provide short-term working capital to exporters.

Export-Import Bank
This bank supports the financing of U.S. goods and services.

Face Value
The amount an issuer agrees to pay upon maturity.

Facility Amount
Total credit facility in place.

Financial Boundaries
Financial statement ratios that a bank requires from a borrower over the term of the loan. See covenants.

Five Cs of Credit
Five characteristics that are used to form a judgement about a customer's creditworthiness: character, capacity, capital, collateral, and conditions.

Fixed Charge
Current fixed obligations on a cash basis.

Fixed Charge Coverage Ratio (FCC)
A measure often used to determine probablility of default. Defined as (EBITDA. - CAPEX - Taxes) / (Interest + Principal).

Fixed Expenses
Expenses that remain the same regardless of production or sales volume in contrasts with Variable Expenses.

Fixed Interest Rate
The fixed percentage paid for borrowing money.

Float
1. The time between the deposit of checks in a bank and when the amount is truly accessible; 2. The amount of funds represented by checks that have been written but not yet presented for payment. Some entries will 'play the float' by writing checks altho

Float Days
The period of time payments are remitted to a lender until the funds are actually credited by the lender through automated clearinghouse procedures. Also known as a Clearance Period.

Floating Rate Note
Security whose coupon rate fluctuates in line with a benchmark interest rate.

Flotation Costs
The total costs of issuing and selling a public security.

Forward Rate Lock
Allows a client to "lock in" a certain interest rate for settlement on a specified date in the future.

Funded Amount
Credit used at a particular time.

Funded Debt
Debt maturing after more than one year.

Growth Capital
External capital inflow to the firm that is intended for expansion of the business, rather than for working capital or refinancing purposes.

Industrial Revenue Bonds
Municipal bonds whose proceeds are loaned to private persons or businesses to finance capital investment projects.

Intercreditor Agreement
An agreement between all lenders on a deal that delineates who owns what rights and when they get paid.

Interest
The price paid for the borrowing money

Interest Rate
The percentage paid for borrowing money.

Interest Rate Cap
Sets a maximum boundary, or limit, on a given floating interest rate.

Interest Rate Collar
Sets a maximum and minimum boundary on a given floating interest rate.

Interest Rate Hedges
Methods by which interest rates are offset, or controlled, by the borrower for a price

Interest Tax Shield
The reductions in income taxes that result from the tax-deductibility of interest payments.

Invested Capital
The sum of equity and debt in a business enterprise.

Investee
Entity that receives capital.

Issue
In securities, issue is stock or bonds sold by a corporation or a government; or, the selling of new securities by a corporation or government through an underwriter or private placement.

Issuer
Company offering securities.

Letter of Credit
A written agreement issued by the bank and given to the seller at the request of the buyer to pay up to a stated sum of money.

Leverage
The use of debt to improve the financial performance of an enterprise. Can also specifically refer to an accounting ratio that measure the proportion of debt in the capital structure of a company, such as the debt/equity ratio.

Leveraged Recapitalization
When a company takes on significant debt in order to pay dividends or repurchase stock. See Equity Recapitalization.

LIBOR
The London Interbank Offered Rate; the rate of interest that major international banks in London charge each other for borrowings.

Lien
A security interest in one or more assets that is granted to lenders in connection with secured debt financing.

Line of Credit
An agreement whereby a financial institution promises to lend up to a certain amount without the need to file another loan application.

Liquidated Collateral
Likely cash value of collateral in liquidation.

Loan Covenant
Agreements between lenders and borrowers requiring the borrowers to follow certain guidelines over the term of the loan.

Loan Guaranty
Percentage of a loan that the SBA or other government agency guarantees.

Long-Term Liabilities
Liabilities of a business due in more than one year. An example of
a long-term liability would be mortgage payable.

Maturity
The date when a loan must be repaid.

Mezzanine Debt
Subordinated debt that provides borrowing capability beyond
senior debt while minimizing the dilution associated with equity
capital. Relies on the coupon for its primary source of return.

Monitoring
Surveillance of a borrower by the bank to ensure the loan is being
used properly.

Negative Covenant
Agreements that restrict the actions of the corporation and
ownership during the term of the loan. If the borrower takes that
certain prohibited action, they will be in breach.

Optimal Capital Structure
The capital structure at which firm value is maximized.

Payment-In-Kind (PIK)
Debt that gives the issuer an option (during an initial period)
either to make coupon payments in cash or in the form of
additional bonds.

Penny Warrants
Warrant that has a nominal price to the investor.

Perfected First Lien
A first lien that is duly recorded with the cognizant governmental
body so that the lender will be able to act on it should to borrower
default.

Personal Guarantee
Collateral security over personally owned assets.

Points
Finance charges paid by the borrower at the beginning of a loan in addition to monthly interest; each point equals one percent of the loan amount.

Prepayment Fees
Penalties to the borrower for terminating a loan before the term expires.

Prime Premium
The premium one pays for borrowing at the Prime Rate rather than LIBOR.

Prime Rate
The interest rate banks have historically charged their most creditworthy customers.

Principal
(1) The total amount of money being borrowed or lent. (2) The party affected by agent decisions in a principal-agent relationship.

Private Capital Markets
Markets where private debt and equity are raised and exchanged.

Private Debt
Technically this is any borrowing done by a company that is not a public bond issue. It more typically refers to debt placed directly with investors or hedge funds.

Promissory Note
Written promise to pay.

Public Markets
Markets where public debt and equity are raised and exchanged.

Restrictive Covenants
Provisions that place constraints on the operations of borrowers, such as restrictions on working capital, fixed assets, future borrowing, and payment of dividend.

Revolver
A loan that can be drawn down and repaid.

Risk Rating
System used by banks to determine a company's risk profile.

Second Lien Debt
Debt that is subordinate to senior debt. If the case of bankruptcy, the senior debt is paid first, then the second lien debt, which is often called mezzanine debt.

Secured Debt
Debt that, in the even of default, has first claim on specified assets.

Security Interest
The right of the creditor to take property or a portion of property offered as security.

Self-Canceling Installment Note (SCIN)
Note that terminates upon some event, usually the death of the payee.

Senior Debt
Debt that, in the even of a bankruptcy, must be repaid before subordinated debt receives any payment.

Senior Debt Lending Multiple
The ratio of senior debt to EBITDA

Seniority
The order of repayment. In the even of a bankruptcy, senior debt must be repaid before subordinated debt.

Simple Interest
Interest computed on principle alone, as opposed to compound interest which includes accrued interest in the calculation.

Stated Interest Rate
Interest rate before applying the "terms cost".

Structured Debt
Debt that has been customized for the buyer, often by
incorporating unusual options.

Subordinated Debt
Debt over which senior debt takes priority.

Subordination
Process that determines which layer of debt has priority in a
bankruptcy.

Swap
An arrangement whereby two companies lend to each other on
different terms, e.g. in different currencies, and/or at different
interest rates, fixed or floating.

Swap Rates
Rate agreed upon between two parties exchanging short-term
payments for long-term payments.

Syndication
The co-investment of different capital providers in a single
company.

Term Loan
Loan typically used to finance fixed-asset purchases.

Terms Cost
Cost of a financing beyond the stated interest rate.

Trade Credit
Credit granted by a firm to another firm for the purchase of goods
or services.

Tranche
Is the piece, portion or slice of a deal or structured financing.
Tranches have distinctive features which for economic or legal
purposes must be financially engineered or structured in order to
conform to prevailing requirements.

Uniform Commercial Code (UCC)
When a lender receives a personal guarantee from a borrower, the lender will often file a UCC lien against the individual assets of the borrower, which prevents the borrower from selling those assets while the debt is still in place.

Unitranche Debt
The combination of senior debt and mezzanine debt into a single loan package.

Unsecured Debt
Debt that does not identify specific assets that can be taken over by the debtholder.

Unused Line Fee
A negotiated fee that is some percentage of the difference between a facility amount and the funded amount.

Variable Interest Rate
The variable percentage paid for borrowing money.

Venture Debt
Lessors that provide equipment to startup and early stage companies.

Warrant
A security entitling the holder to buy a proportionate amount of stock at some specified future date at a specified price, usually one higher than current market.

Mergers & Acquisitions Terms

Accretive
Growth by gradual addition. In finance, an action is accretive if it adds to earnings per share.

Acquiree
The firm being purchased in an acquisition. See Target.

Acquirer
A firm or individual that is purchasing an equity interest in another company.

Acquisition of Assets
A merger or consolidation in which an acquirer purchases the selling firm's assets without getting any ownership of the company itself.

Acquisition of Stock
A merger or consolidation in which an acquirer purchases the acquirer's stock.

Add-On Acquisition
A horizontal purchase of similar company that increases the size of or compliments the platform company.

BIMBO
Buy/In Management Buyout. Transaction in which business is bought out by a management team comprised of existing and incoming management.

BIO
Institutional buyout where an equity sponsor introduces new management.

Bizcomps
Database published semi-annually chronicling numerous transactions in different regions, each with approximately 20 data points of information with which to use in valuations under $5 million.

Bolt-On Acquisition
A horizontal acquisition that is done primarily to increase the size (revenue) of the platform company.

Breakup Fee
Penalty paid to the acquiror if the target backs out of the deal. See Termination Fee.

Business Broker
One who works with buyers or sellers of small businesses to help them with their transaction.

Business Transfer
The spectrum of possibilities, from transferring assets of a company to transferring partial or full enterprise stock interests.

Buy and Build
Method of consolidation that uses private equity and debt for the initial acquisition of the platform company, then for the additional bolt-on acquisitions.

Buy/Sell Agreement
A binding contract between the various owners of a business that controls when an owner can sell his interest, to whom and for how much.

Buyout
Purchase of a controlling interest (or percent of shares) of a company's stock. A leveraged buy-out is done with borrowed money.

Call for Offers
Made by the intermediary of a private auction after buyer visits to gain a better perspective of the potential suitors.

Change in Control Provision
Protects an employee from adverse effects if the ownership of the company changes.

Confidentiality Agreement
Nondisclosure agreement between buyer and seller.

Consolidation
The initial acquisition of one or more platform companies, followed by the purchase of add-on acquisitions.

Consolidation
A period where there is intensive merger activity within an industry resulting in a measurably reduced number of firms in that industry.

Corporate Acquisition
The acquisition of one firm by another firm.

Cost Savings Synergy
Synergy that results from expenses that are no longer needed when business functions are consolidated.

Culture
The behaviors and values of a company that make it unique. Incompatible cultures are a common cause of integration problems with mergers.

Data Room
Area containing mass amounts of information regarding the subject of an auction.

Deal Sourcing
The process of finding acquisition target candidates in M&A and private equity.

Dilutive
In finance, an action is dilutive if it results in decreased earnings per share.

Drag Along Rights
Entitlement of the majority stakeholder to force a minority stakeholder to join a transaction where it is selling its stake.

Dry Powder
Metaphorically refers to dry gunpowder, meaning that the possessor of dry powder has the ability to continue to fight. In finance, this means that the investor still has a cash reserve with which to make additional investments.

Due Diligence
The discovery and examination period after execution of a letter of intent.

Dutch Auction
An auction where the bidding starts at a high price and then the auctioneer incrementally lowers the price until it reaches a point where the entire offering is sold.

Earn-Out
Method for triggering changes in the purchase price based on future performance of the subject company. The seller "earns" a portion of the purchase price by the company meeting ageed-upon future performance milestones.

Employment Agreement
Agreement that sets the terms for continued employment upon the closing of a buyout.

Equity Penalties
Agreements that increase an investor's percentage of ownership upon the occurrence of a certain event.

Equity Sponsor
Private equity provider that finances a buyout for a management team.

Equity Sponsored Buyout
A management team partners with an equity sponsor (provider) to perform a buyout.

Expression of Interest
Document signed by the top prospects in an auction that narrows attention to the best suitors.

Features
Characteristics of a particular security such as whether or not it is convertible, redeemable, exchangeable, etc.

Financial Buyer
A buyer that is intending to buy the company, hold for a period of time, then sell. The alternative is a strategic buyer that wants to integrate the target company into their long-term strategy.

Financial Control Premium
Control value of an enterprise based on financial returns.

Forced Liquidation Value
Estimated gross amount of money that could be realized from sale in public auction, or negotiated liquidation sale with seller having a sense of immediacy.

Going Concern
An ongoing operating business enterprise

Going Concern Assumption
Assumption that a business will remain in operation indefinitely.

Going Concern Value
The value of a business enterprise that is expected to continue to operate into the future.

Gross Margin Enhancements
Synergy benefit that occurs when one party's gross margin is
improved due to another party's efficiency in the production cycle.

Holding Company
A company which owns or controls other companies.

Horizontal Integration
Merger or acquisition involving two or more firms in the same
industry in the same position in the supply chain.

Human Capital
The combined knowledge, skill, innovativeness, and ability of the
company's individual employees to meet the task at hand.

Idemnification
Immunity from financial or legal liability.

IMAP
International Network of M&A Partners. A worldwide group of
investment bankers that advise in the sale of private companies.

Investment Horizon
Timeframe within which an investor will exit an investment.

Letter of Intent
A legally nonbinding agreement that describes the important terms
of a deal.

Leveraged Buyout (LBO)
The use of borrowed money to finance the purchase of a firm.

M&A Intermediary
Firm that focuses on providing merger, acquisition, and divestiture
services to middle market companies.

Majority Interest
An ownership interest greater than fifty percent (50%) of the
voting interest in a business enterprise.

Management Buy-In
Purchase of an ownership interest by a management team not currently involved in the business.

Management Buyout
Buyout by existing management of part or all of the ownership of the company.

Merger
The union of two or more commercial interests or corporations.

Milestones
Included in the term sheet, they set forth certain benchmarks for the company, with corresponding staged investments.

Negotiated Transfer
Transfer method where the parties work out a deal.

No Shop
Period stipulated in a letter of intent within which the company or its agents cannot solicit other investor interest.

Non-Strategic Transfer
A transfer involving a buyer not strategic to the business.

One-Step Auction
Auction that concurrently encourages interest within a limited group of buyers.

Pipeline
The list of potential deals that are in development but typically not yet engaged.

Private Auction
Selling process in which an intermediary simultaneously contacts a limited number of prospects in an attempt to confidentially maximize the selling price.

Public Auction
Auction where confidentiality is not important and selling price is a function of a bidding war.

Ratchets
Device to encourage management to perform against defined targets. Can also refer to mechanisms that prevent dilution of equity positions of current investors by future investors.

Repurchase Agreements
Buy/Sell agreement in which an existing entity buys a business interest from an exiting party.

Retention Plan
The plan by the acquirer to retain key personnel of the target firm post-acquisition.

Russian Roulette
Buy/Sell agreement in which the exiting party sets a share price for the stock and a period. If the stock is not bought by existing owners in the period, they may offer the exiting party their shareholdings at the originally stated price.

Seller Financing
The seller of a business provides financing to the buyer for the transaction.

Selling Memorandum
Document that disseminates information to potential buyers during an auction.

Specific Investor Return
An acquirer's expected rate of return.

Strategic Buyer
An acquirer that intends to keep the new company as part of its long-term strategy.

Strategic Combinations
Synergies that arise from strategic motives.

Strategic Control Value
Value of 100% of the company based on strategic or synergistic considerations.

Synergistic Buyer
The strategic acquirer in a synergistic relationship. See Strategic Buyer.

Synergy
The increase in performance of the combined firm over what the two firms are expected to accomplish as independent companies.

Tag Along Rights
Entitlement of minority stakeholder to join a transaction if the majority chooses to sell its stake.

Target
Company sought by an acquirer.

Termination Fee
Penalty paid to the acquiror if the target backs out of the deal. See Breakup Fee.

Triggering Events
Events that activate a buy/sell agreement.

Two-Step Auction
Each step of the selling process is staged using deadlines.

Vertical Integration
Merger in which one firm acquires another firm that is in the same industry but at another position in the supply chain.

Vesting
The "earning" of stock by founders or key employees upon continued employment.

Asset-Based Lending & Factoring Ter

Advance Rates
The ratio relationship between the amount of money a lender extends and the value of the pledged collateral.

Air-Ball
The portion of an asset-based loan that is not covered by the collateral.

Asset-Based Lending (ABL)
Debt that is secured by assets such as inventory, accounts receivable, real estate, etc.

Blocked Account
Account controlled by the lender while payments are remitted during a clearance period.

Clearance Period
See Float Days

Commission
Fee to the factor that covers the credit process that a client wishes the factor to perform.

Debtor
1) In lending, it is the borrower. 2) In factoring, it is the entity that generates the receivable.

Discount Fee
Factoring charge that involves two costs: a commission charge, and an interest rate for the cash advances.

Eligible Assets
Assets that qualify for advances on an asset based loan.

Factoring
The process of purchasing accounts receivable at a discount.

Fee Clock
Timeframe for charges owed to the factor once it receives the invoice from the client.

Invoice
An itemized list of goods shipped usually specifying the price and the terms of sale.

Liquidated Collateral
Likely cash value of collateral in liquidation.

Loan-to-Value Ratio
See Advance Rates.

Margined Collateral
The result of an advance rate applied against a qualifying asset.

Maturity Factoring
An account receivable item is purchased on the date payment is due on the account.

Merchant Cash Advance
The purchase of a company's future credit card purchases at a discount. Similar to factoring.

Nonmaturity Factoring
Factor purchases invoice upon shipment receipt.

Non-Recourse Factoring
A factor has no claim against the client if the debtor defaults.

Recourse Factoring
The factor establishes how long it will wait to be paid until the accounts receivable reverts back to the client.

Reserve
The invoice amount minus the advance plus the fee, which a factor holds until it rebates the client.

Investor/Limited Partner Terms

2/20 Fee Model
An investment fund where investors pay a 2% management fee plus 20% carried interest (aka incentive fee).

Accredited Investor
Investors who are considered by the SEC to be wealthy enough to afford to lose their investment in a worse case scenario. A single person is an accredited investor if he/she has $200,000 in annual income or a net worth of more than $1 million (excluding residence).

Alternative Investment
Investments other than cash or publicly traded stocks and bonds. Generally illiquid and require the investor to be an accredited investor. Can include real estate (and other real assets), hedge funds, angel investments, venture capital, private equity, and private debt.

Angel Investor
Wealthy investor that participates in high-risk deals with early stage companies.

Burn-Out Round
This is a venture capital funding round for a company that is not doing well, so the share price is very low (a down round) which means that the new infusion of capital results in a high level of dilution of the stakes of the investors in prior rounds. Also known as wash-out round or a cram-down round.

Carried Interest
A percentage of an investment fund's capital gains that is paid to the fund's general partner. See incentive fee.

Catch-Up

An alternative investment fund fee structure where there is an overall incentive fee even when there is a hurdle rate in place. Thus, as soon as the hurdle rate is satisfied, the fund enters a "catch-up" phase, where all additional gains to go the general partner until the point is reached where the overall incentive fee percentage has been paid. After that, gains are split between the general partner and limited partners according to the normal schedule.

Clawback

A provision in an alternative investment fund fee structure where the general partner must refund a portion of incentive fees paid on early harvesting activities if later lower fund performance doesn't justify those incentive fees overall.

Co-Investment

An opportunity offered to a limited partner to make a direct investment (outside of the fund) to a fund's portfolio company.

Committed Capital

The amount that has been pledged to an investment fund by investors, but not yet paid to the fund.

Dry Powder

Metaphorically refers to dry gunpowder, meaning that the possessor of dry powder has the ability to continue to fight. In finance, this means that the investor still has a cash reserve with which to make additional investments.

Family Office

An entity whose sole activity is managing the trusts and investments of a single family.

Hedge Fund
Historically, an alternative investment fund using publicly traded derivatives to limit downside investment risk. Now, hedge funds can generically refer to nearly any investment strategy that uses a limited partnership fund structure.

Independent Sponsor
A private equity investor that invests their own funds directly rather than as a limited partner in an investment fund. (a.k.a Fundless Sponsor).

Institutional Investor
An entity, company, mutual fund, insurance corporation, brokerage, or other such group that invests.

Investor's Rights
Privileges of the investor outlined in the term sheet.

Limited Partner
A partner who has limited legal liability for the obligations of the partnership.

Offeree
Investor to whom securities are offered.

Oversubscribed
When during the fundraising phase of an investment fund, the fundraising goal is exceeded.

Preemptive Rights
The rights of the investor to acquire new securities issued by the company to the extent necessary to maintain its percentage interest on a converted basis.

Preferred Return
The return that an investment fund must achieve before carried interest is paid to the general partner. A common level for the preferred return is around 8%. See Hurdle Rate.

Private Return Expectation
The expected rate of return that the private capital markets require in order to attract funds to a particular investment. .

Skin-In-The-Game
In private equity, refers to the general partner of a fund investing its own money in the fund as a limited partner. This shows alignment with the interests of the investors.

Specific Industry Return
The average expected return for investors in companies within a certain industry.

Specific Investor Return
An acquirer's expected rate of return.

Undersubscribed
At the end of the fundraising phase of an investment fund, the fundraising goal is has not been achieved.

Visitation
Right of investors to attend board meetings and meet with management on a periodic basis.

Leasing Terms

Bank Lessors
When a bank provides the equipment lease, rather than a finance company or the equipment vendor.

Bargain-Purchase-Price-Option
Gives the lessee the options to purchases the asset at a price below fair market value when the lease expires.

Captive Lessors
Subsidiaries of manufacturers that provide financing to customers in the form of an equipment lease.

Equipment Leasing
Commercial finance provider that provide lease funding for equipment used in the operations of a business.

Finance Lease
Noncancellable lease which requires the lessee to remit payments of lease rentals that total the cost of the asset plus the lessor's required profit.

Independent Lessors
General leasing companies that may be affiliated with a larger finance company.

Lease Factor
A mathematical expression that describes the lease payment as a decimal/fraction of the equipment acquisition cost.

Lessee
An entity that leases an asset from another entity.

Lessor
An entity that leases an asset to another entity.

Master Lease
An agreement that consolidates individual lease transactions into a single leasing program.

Operating Lease
Lease extended for small part of the useful life of the equipment. Lessor expected to return the equipment after term.

Residual Value
Value remaining in equipment after lease term has expired.

Sale-Leaseback
Sale of an existing asset to a financial institution that then leases it back to the user.

Salvage Value
Scrap value of plant and equipment.

Specialty Lessors
Lessors that specialize in an industry or with certain types of equipment

True Lease
Lease in which the lessor takes the risk of ownership and, as owner, is entitled to the benefits of ownership, such as tax benefits.

Leadership & Governance Terms

Block Voting
A group of shareholders banding together to vote their shares into a single block.

Change in Control Provision
Protects an employee from adverse effects if the ownership of the company changes.

Contribution to Profits Method
Method of deriving amount of Key Person Insurance that multiplies the excess profit attributed to that employee by the number of years it will take to train someone to fill the vacant position.

Control
The power to direct the management and policies of a business enterprise.

Control Premium
An amount by which the pro rata value of a controlling interest exceeds the pro rata value of a noncontrolling interest in a business enterprise that reflects the power of control.

Cost of Replacement Method
Method of deriving amount of Key Person Insurance that calculates the direct costs required to interview, hire, and train a replacement, as well as the opportunity costs incurred due to the loss of the key employee.

Dissent
Action taken by minority shareholders who believe the majority has taken corporate actions that negatively affect them.

Division
A self-sufficient unit within a company.

Dodd-Frank
Refers to The Dodd-Frank Wall Street Reform and Consumer Protection Act, passed in 2010. Implemented additional monitoring for financial institutions deemed "too big to fail" and imposed additional restrictions on lending to consumers. Also imposed the Volcker Rule to limit speculative trading by banks.

Employment Agreement
Agreement that sets the terms for continued employment upon the closing of a buyout.

Exit Strategy
Investor insistence on certain rights so they may realize the value of their investment if they see fit to exit.

Governance
The way in which major financial and legal issues of the company will be managed as presented in the term sheet.

Human Capital
The combined knowledge, skill, innovativeness, and ability of the company's individual employees to meet the task at hand.

Insider
Directors, officers, and others in a corporation who know of or have access to confidential information that has not been released to the general public.

Key Person
Important person without whom a company can expect to experience a decrease in future income.

Key Person Discount
An amount or percentage deducted from the value of an ownership interest to reflect the reduction in value resulting from the actual or potential loss of a key person in a business enterprise.

Nonvoting Shares
Common shares with no voting rights.

Operating Partner
A member of the management team of a private equity fund who works directly with the portfolio companies to increase value.

Organic Growth
Company growth fueled solely by retained earnings rather than by outside investment.

Perquisite
Personal benefits accruing to owners or employees of a business that is derived from sources other than wages.

Phantom Stock
Right to a bonus based upon the performance of shares of a corporation's common stock (without actually receiving those shares) over a specified period of time.

Principal
(1) The total amount of money being borrowed or lent. (2) The party affected by agent decisions in a principal-agent relationship.

Sarbanes-Oxley
The Sarbanes-Oxley Act of 2002. Also called Sarbox or SOX. Expanded compliance requirements and penalties for boards of directors, management and public accountants as a response to the accounting fraud scandals at Enron and Worldcom.

Sole Proprietorship
A business owned by a single individual.

Stakeholders
All parties that have an interest, financial or otherwise, in a firm. Includes stockholders, creditors, bondholders, employees, customers, management, the community, and the government.

Stock Appreciation Rights
Rights granted to employees to receive a benefit equal to the appreciation of a given number of shares over a specified period.

Succession Plan
The founder's plan to eventually replace the founding senior management team with professionals.

Supermajority
Provision in a company's charter requiring a majority of, say, 80% of shareholders to approve certain changes, such as a merger.

Tie-Break Director
Director appointed by partners to settle a decision in the event of a deadlock.

Vesting
The "earning" of stock by founders or key employees upon continued employment.

Visitation
Right of investors to attend board meetings and meet with management on a periodic basis.

Voting Rights
The rights to vote on matters that are put to a vote of security holders.

Public Market Terms

American Stock Exchange (AMEX)
The third-largest stock exchange in the United States. It trades mostly in small-to-medium-sized companies. It is owned by the New York Stock Exchange (NYSE).

Arbitrage
A technique employed to profit from buying or selling the same security in different market places, thus making money from the disparity in market prices.

Blockage Discount
An amount or percentage deducted from the current market price of a publicly traded security to reflect the decrease in the per share value of a block of those securities that is of a size that could not be sold in a reasonable period of time given normal trading volume.

Bulletin Board
Electronic quotation system that displays real-time quotes, last sale prices, and volume information for many over the counter stocks.

Could-Be-Public Companies
Private companies with similar characteristics to those of public companies.

Direct Public Offering
Do-It-Yourself IPO where the registration of the securities with the regulators is accomplished using simplified forms and procedures, such as the SCOR offering.

EDGAR
The Securities & Exchange Commission Electronic Data Gathering and Retrieval to transmit company documents such as 10-Ks, 10-Qs, quarterly reports, and other SEC filings, to investors.

Efficient Market
A market in which new information is available to all parties and is very quickly reflected accurately in asset prices.

Equity Risk Premium
The amount that investors are compensated for assuming nondiversifiable equity risk.

Exchange
The venue or trading activity between market participants.

Financial Engineer
One who combines or divides existing financial methods or instruments to create new financial products or services.

Going Private
Publicly owned stock is replaced with complete equity ownership by a private group.

Going Public
Undergoing an initial public offering.

Initial Public Offering (IPO)
A company's first sale of stock to the public.

Market Maker
Firm that stands ready to buy and sell a particular stock on a regular and continuous basis at a publicly quoted price.

Marketable Minority Interest
Minority interest assumed to be freely tradable in the marketplace.

NASDAQ
National Association of Securities Dealers Automated Quotations.

New York Stock Exchange (NYSE)
Also known as the Big Board or the Exchange. More than 2,000 common and preferred stocks are traded. The exchange is the oldest and largest in the United States. It is located on Wall Street in New York City.

Over-the-Counter (OTC)
A computerized network (NASDAQ) through which trades of bonds, non-listed stocks, and other securities take place.

Pink Sheets
Listings of price quotes for companies that trade in the over the counter market.

Poof IPO
See Roll-Up

Pre-IPO Studies
Conducted to determine a stock's marketability discount upon initial offering.

Price/Earnings Ratio
Shows the "multiple" of earnings at which a public stock sells.

Public Guideline Companies
Public companies used in the valuation of a private company due to the comparative qualities between them.

Public Markets
Markets where public debt and equity are raised and exchanged.

Quiet Period
Time between the filing of a Registration Statement and its acceptance by the SEC.

Red Herring
A preliminary registration statement describing the issue (the IPO) and prospects of the company that must be filed with the SEC or provincial securities commission.

Registration Rights
Rights that govern the how a company goes public, who pays the cost associated with the process, and how many times it can file an IPO.

Regulation A
The securities regulation that exempts small public offerings, those valued at less than $5 million, from most registration requirements with the SEC.

Regulation D
A series of six rules, Rules 501-506, establishing transactional exemptions from the registration requirements of the 1933 Act.

Reverse Merger
A private company goes public by purchasing a public company shell, then using that shell to acquire the original private company.

Roll-Up
Simultaneous consolidation and initial public offering.

SCOR
Small Corporate Offering Registration. An "IPO-Lite" available under Reg A with reduced documentation and disclosures.

Secondary Market
The exchange or over-the-counter market where shares are traded after the initial offering.

Shell Company
Existing public company in a reverse merger.

Should-Be-Private Company
Company whose costs of being public outweigh its benefits.

Stock Exchanges
Formal organizations, approved and regulated by the Securities & Exchange Commission (SEC), that are made up of members that use the facilities to exchange certain common stocks.

Stock Market
Also called the equity market, the market for trading equities.

Government, Tax & Regulatory Terms

7(a) Loan Guaranty Program
SBA program that provides loan guarantees to small businesses unable to secure financing on reasonable terms through normal lending channels. Maximum loan is $5 million and loan term is 25 years for real estate, 10 years for equipment and 7 years for working capital. 7(a) loans are fully amortized.

Black-Scholes
A model for pricing call options that uses the stock price, the exercise price, the risk-free interest rate, the time to expiration, and the standard deviation of the historical return of the underlying stock.

Business & Industry Loans
Loans provided to rural companies with stipulation that a job must be created or retained for each $40,000 loaned.

CAPLine Program
Umbrella program under which the SBA helps small businesses meet their short-term and cyclical working capital needs.

Certified Development Company 504 Program
SBA program that provides growing businesses with long-term fixed-rate financing for major fixed assets, such as land and buildings.

Contribution to Profits Method
Method of deriving amount of Key Person Insurance that multiplies the excess profit attributed to that employee by the number of years it will take to train someone to fill the vacant position.

Cost of Replacement Method
Method of deriving amount of Key Person Insurance that
calculates the direct costs required to interview, hire, and train a
replacement, as well as the opportunity costs incurred due to the
loss of the key employee.

Default Risk
The risk that a company will be unable to pay the principal or
contractual interest on its debt obligations.

Dodd-Frank
Refers to The Dodd-Frank Wall Street Reform and Consumer
Protection Act, passed in 2010. Implemented additional
monitoring for financial institutions deemed "too big to fail" and
imposed additional restrictions on lending to consumers. Also
imposed the Volcker Rule to limit speculative trading by banks.

EDGAR
The Securities & Exchange Commission Electronic Data
Gathering and Retrieval to transmit company documents such as
10-Ks, 10-Qs, quarterly reports, and other SEC filings, to
investors.

ERISA
Employee Retirement Income Security Act of 1974.

Estate Tax
A tax imposed by a state or the federal government on assets left to
heirs in a will.

Export Working Capital Program
SBA program designed to provide short-term working capital to
exporters.

Export-Import Bank
This bank supports the financing of U.S. goods and services.

FASB
Financial Accounting Standards Board

Federal Reserve System
The central bank of the U.S., established in 1913, and governed by the Federal Reserve Board located in Washington, D.C.

Financial Accounting Standards Board (FASB)
An accounting oversight committee that sets accounting standards for U.S. firms.

Fiscal Policy
Government policy regarding taxation and spending. Fiscal policy is made by Congress and Administration.

Future
Agreement between two parties to perform a trade in the future at a fixed price.

Futures
A term used to designate all contracts covering the sale of financial instruments or physical commodities for future delivery on a commodity exchange.

Generally Accepted Accounting Principles (GAAP)
A technical accounting term that encompasses the conventions, rules, and procedures necessary to define accepted accounting practice at a particular time.

Hedge
A term to describe protective maneuvering by an investment manager to reduce the risk of a loss from a specified event.

Interest Rate Hedges
Methods by which interest rates are offset, or controlled, by the borrower for a price

IRS Published Interest Rate
Benchmark interest rate set forth by the IRS.

Letter Stock
Privately placed common stock, so-called because the SEC requires a letter from the purchaser stating that the stock is not intended for resale.

Loan Guaranty
Percentage of a loan that the SBA or other government agency guarantees.

Lost Profits
Commercial damages due to a business interruption.

MACRS
Modified accelerated cost recovery system.

Multiple Compensation Method
Method of deriving amount of Key Person Insurance that multiplies that employee's compensation by the number of years it will take to train someone to fill the vacant position.

Option
Gives the buyer the right, but not the obligation, to buy or sell an asset at a set price on or before a given date.

Option Price
Also called the option premium, the price paid by the buyer of the options contract for the right to buy or sell a security at a specified price in the future.

Period of Restoration
The theoretical reasonable amount of time that it should take the insured to repair the damage of the business interruption and resume operations.

Quiet Period
Time between the filing of a Registration Statement and its acceptance by the SEC.

Red Herring
A preliminary registration statement describing the issue (the IPO) and prospects of the company that must be filed with the SEC or provincial securities commission.

Registration Statement
Legal document filed with the SEC to register securities for public offering.

Regulation
The attempt to bring the market under the control of an authority.

Regulation A+
An SEC regulation that allows companies to raise up to $50MM from both accredited and non-accredited investors. Companies that do this are called a Mini-IPO.

Revenue Ruling 59-60
U.S. Treasury Department ruling that outlines procedures for determining fair market value of private companies.

Risk
Degree of uncertainty of return on an asset. Often defined as the standard deviation of the return on total investment.

Rule 504
A business using this Reg. D offering can raise a maximum of $1 million less the total dollar amount of securities sold during the preceding twelve month period under Rule 504.

Rule 505
This Reg. D offering may not exceed $5 million less the total dollar amount of securities sold during the preceding twelve month period under Rule 504, Rule 505 or Section 3(b) of the Act.

Rule 506
This Reg. D offering provides an exemption for limited offers and sales without regard to the dollar amount of the offering.

Safe Harbor Rule
SEC Rule 147, which allows companies to raise money without registering as a public company as long as they are incorporated, do business, and solicit investors all within a single US state.

Sarbanes-Oxley
The Sarbanes-Oxley Act of 2002. Also called Sarbox or SOX. Expanded compliance requirements and penalties for boards of directors, management and public accountants as a response to the accounting fraud scandals at Enron and Worldcom.

SBIC
Small business investment company.

Securities & Exchange Commission (SEC)
Federal agency that regulates U.S. financial markets.

Securities Act of 1933
Requires companies offering securities to the public to be registered with the US Government.

Securities Act of 1934
Established the Securities & Exchange Commission (SEC) and regulates the secondary markets or exchanges.

Single Life Annuity
Private annuity whose payments stop with the death of the seller.

Small Business Administration (SBA)
Government organization that provides financial, technical, and management assistance to help Americans start, run, and grow their businesses.

Small Business Investment Company (SBIC)
Government-sponsored entity that invests in small businesses.

Spin-Off
When a large enterprise takes one of its divisions and makes it a stand-alone company.

Swap
An arrangement whereby two companies lend to each other on different terms, e.g. in different currencies, and/or at different interest rates, fixed or floating.

Swap Rates
Rate agreed upon between two parties exchanging short-term payments for long-term payments.

Uniform Commercial Code (UCC)
When a lender receives a personal guarantee from a borrower, the lender will often file a UCC lien against the individual assets of the borrower, which prevents the borrower from selling those assets while the debt is still in place.

Volcker Rule
A rule under Dodd-Frank that limits proprietary trading of securities by banks.

Business Transfer Terms

Annual Exclusion Gifts
Gifts of up to $11,000 to an unlimited number of recipients that do not incur taxes.

BIMBO
Buy/In Management Buyout. Transaction in which business is bought out by a management team comprised of existing and incoming management.

BIO
Institutional buyout where an equity sponsor introduces new management.

Business Transfer
The spectrum of possibilities, from transferring assets of a company to transferring partial or full enterprise stock interests.

Charitable Lead Annuity Trust
Trust that distributes a certain amount to a beneficiary at least annually for a term of years.

Charitable Lead Trust
Irrevocable trust that income to a charity for a specified period of time. Income interest to the charity must be either annuity interest or unitrust interest.

Charitable Lead Unitrust
Trust that distributes a fixed percentage of the net fair market value of its assets valued annually.

Charitable Remainder Annuity Trust
CRT that pays a fixed dollar amount or a fixed percentage of the initial fair market value of the CRT assets.

Charitable Remainder Trust
Irrevocable trust in which one or more individuals are paid income until the grantor's death, at which time the balance becomes tax free and is passed on to a designated charity.

Charitable Remainder Unitrust
Trust that pays a fixed percentage of the CRT assets valued annually.

Donor
Individual who donates property to another through a trust. Also called a grantor.

Early Equity Value
The value of a business interest as a startup, often prior to profit or even revenue.

Employee Stock Ownership Plan (ESOP)
A company contributes to a trust fund that buys stock on behalf of employees.

Engineered Intra-Transfers
Custom-tailored solutions designed to transfer all or part of the business internally.

Equity Sponsor
Private equity provider that finances a buyout for a management team.

Equity Sponsored Buyout
A management team partners with an equity sponsor (provider) to perform a buyout.

ERISA
Employee Retirement Income Security Act of 1974.

ESOP Tax Deferral
The ability to sell stock to a Trust and defer or permanently avoid taxation on any gain resulting from the sale.

Estate
All the assets a person possesses at the time of death, including securities, real estate, interest in business, physical possessions, and cash.

Estate Freeze
The seller freezes the value of the business at the date of transfer, and the grantee benefits from the appreciation of the stock thereafter.

Estate Tax
A tax imposed by a state or the federal government on assets left to heirs in a will.

Family Limited Partnership
Limited partnership in which only family members are included as partners.

Forced Liquidation Value
Estimated gross amount of money that could be realized from sale in public auction, or negotiated liquidation sale with seller having a sense of immediacy.

Generation Skipping Tax
Tax on transfers to a grandchild or more remote relative, or a non-family member, who is more than 37 1/2 years younger than the transferor.

Going Concern
An ongoing operating business enterprise

Going Concern Value
The value of a business enterprise that is expected to continue to operate into the future.

Grantee
The person or entity to whom property or assets are transferred. See Beneficiary.

EEF (QR) - Business Transfer Terms

Grantor
The person or entity who transfers property or assets.

Grantor Retained Annuity Trust
Irrevocable trust that pays an annuity to the term holder for a fixed time period.

Grantor Retained Unitrust
The grantor's retained interest is a specified percentage of the trust's fair market value each year, instead of a fixed dollar amount.

Hybrid Agreement
Buy/sell agreement that allows the founder first priority to buy an exiting interest with other owners or partners second in line to purchase.

Intentionally Defective Grantor Trust
Trust that takes stock in exchange for a promissory note. The grantor pays estate tax on the note and accumulated interest but avoids income tax since it sees no gain or loss.

Irrevocable Life Insurance Trust
See Wealth Replacement Trust

Last Survivor Annuity
Private annuity whose payments continue until the death of the last survivor.

Leveraged ESOP
ESOP that borrows money from a lender that is then repaid by the company through tax-deductible contributions to a Trust.

Lifetime Exclusion Gifts
Gifts that may total up to $1 million over the course of one's lifetime without incurring any taxes.

Management Buy-In
Purchase of an ownership interest by a management team not currently involved in the business.

123

Management Buyout
Buyout by existing management of part or all of the ownership of the company.

Negotiated Transfer
Transfer method where the parties work out a deal.

Non-Strategic Transfer
A transfer involving a buyer not strategic to the business.

One-Step Auction
Auction that concurrently encourages interest within a limited group of buyers.

Private Annuities
Transfer of stock in exchange for an unsecured promise to receive a stream of fixed payments for the life of the seller.

Public Auction
Auction where confidentiality is not important and selling price is a function of a bidding war.

Repurchase Agreements
Buy/Sell agreement in which an existing entity buys a business interest from an exiting party.

Russian Roulette
Buy/Sell agreement in which the exiting party sets a share price for the stock and a period. If the stock is not bought by existing owners in the period, they may offer the exiting party their shareholdings at the originally stated price.

Seller Financing
The seller of a business provides financing to the buyer for the transaction.

Stock Gifts
Transference of stock to a family member.

Taxable Gifts
Gifts not exempt from taxation.

Two-Step Auction
Each step of the selling process is staged using deadlines.

Wealth Replacement Trust
Trust that owns a life insurance policy payable upon death to the trust to received by the beneficiary.

Legal Terms

Anti-Assignment Provision
A clause in a contract that prevents the contract from being sold or assigned to a third-party without the consent of all parties. Most relevant in asset sales, where all relevant contracts with vendors and customers must be individually renegotiated.

Arbitration
Process in which both sides of a deadlock present their case to a third party, who makes a binding ruling that both parties have previously committed to abide.

Articles of Incorporation
Legal document establishing a corporation and its structure and purpose.

Bankruptcy
State of being insolvent and thus unable to pay debts.

Blue Sky Laws
Securities laws particular to the individual states.

Boilerplate
Standard terms and conditions. Don't accept these at face value. Hire a securities attorney to review.

Breakup Fee
Penalty paid to the acquiror if the target backs out of the deal. See Termination Fee.

Caps and Baskets
Terms included in the sale agreement. Caps limit the idemnification for the buyer if the seller makes a misrepresentation. Baskets are a monetary hurdle that idemnification claims must exceed before they are payable.

Chapter 11
Voluntary bankruptcy filing by the debtor.

Chapter 7
Involuntary liquidation forced by creditor(s).

Charitable Lead Annuity Trust
Trust that distributes a certain amount to a beneficiary at least annually for a term of years.

Charitable Lead Trust
Irrevocable trust that income to a charity for a specified period of time. Income interest to the charity must be either annuity interest or unitrust interest.

Charitable Lead Unitrust
Trust that distributes a fixed percentage of the net fair market value of its assets valued annually.

Charitable Remainder Annuity Trust
CRT that pays a fixed dollar amount or a fixed percentage of the initial fair market value of the CRT assets.

Charitable Remainder Trust
Irrevocable trust in which one or more individuals are paid income until the grantor's death, at which time the balance becomes tax free and is passed on to a designated charity.

Charitable Remainder Unitrust
Trust that pays a fixed percentage of the CRT assets valued annually.

Confidentiality Agreement
Nondisclosure agreement between buyer and seller.

Copyright
A form of legal protection used to safeguard original literary works, performing arts, sound recordings, visual arts, original software code and renewals. Protected for the life of the author plus 70 years.

Cure Period
A period of time specified in the loan agreement within which the borrower has to mend any violations of the loan covenant.

Design Patent
Protects the original appearance of an article of manufacture, not its structural features. Carries a term of 14 years.

Entity
In business it is a separate or self-contained body that provides goods or services.

ESOP Tax Deferral
The ability to sell stock to a Trust and defer or permanently avoid taxation on any gain resulting from the sale.

Estate
All the assets a person possesses at the time of death, including securities, real estate, interest in business, physical possessions, and cash.

Estate Freeze
The seller freezes the value of the business at the date of transfer, and the grantee benefits from the appreciation of the stock thereafter.

Estate Tax
A tax imposed by a state or the federal government on assets left to heirs in a will.

Family Limited Partnership
Limited partnership in which only family members are included as partners.

Fiduciary
A person, company, or association who is responsible for investing the assets of the beneficiary in a prudent manner.

General Partner
In an FLP, usually the parents or corporation owned by the parents typically holding a nominal partnership interest.

Governance
The way in which major financial and legal issues of the company will be managed as presented in the term sheet.

Grantor Retained Annuity Trust
Irrevocable trust that pays an annuity to the term holder for a fixed time period.

Grantor Retained Unitrust
The grantor's retained interest is a specified percentage of the trust's fair market value each year, instead of a fixed dollar amount.

Holding Company
A company which owns or controls other companies.

Idemnification
Immunity from financial or legal liability.

Insider
Directors, officers, and others in a corporation who know of or have access to confidential information that has not been released to the general public.

Intellectual Property
An original idea or concept of the creator that can be trademarked, patented, copyrighted, or held as a trade secret.

Intentionally Defective Grantor Trust
Trust that takes stock in exchange for a promissory note. The grantor pays estate tax on the note and accumulated interest but avoids income tax since it sees no gain or loss.

Irrevocable Life Insurance Trust
See Wealth Replacement Trust

Last Survivor Annuity
Private annuity whose payments continue until the death of the
last survivor.

Letter of Intent
A legally nonbinding agreement that describes the important terms
of a deal.

Lien
A security interest in one or more assets that is granted to lenders
in connection with secured debt financing.

Limited Liability Company (LLC)
Form of business organization in which each owner of the business
is not liable for the debts of the business unless they have
personally covenanted to accept such an obligation.

Mediation
Process in which a mediator hears both sides of a deadlock and
rules in favor of one. Both sides must agree with the decision in
order to move forward.

Model Business Corporation Act
A model act developed by the American Bar Association to help
modernize and harmonize state laws governing the formation and
operation of corporations.

Non-Advocacy
Stance of indifference an appraiser must take in order to conduct a
fair and unbiased appraisal.

Offering Memorandum
A document that outlines the terms of securities to be offered in a
private placement.

Oppression
Legal term meaning the minority shareholder's reasonable expectations have not been met.

Ownership Agreements
Legal agreements that define the rights and privileges of the owners.

Pari Passu
Pari Passu translates as "without partiality" from Latin. It is used in reference to two classes of securities or obligations that have equal entitlement to payment.

Patent
The grant of a property right by the U.S. government to the inventor by action of the Patent and Trademark office.

Perfected First Lien
A first lien that is duly recorded with the cognizant governmental body so that the lender will be able to act on it should to borrower default.

Private Placement Memorandum (PPM)
Document that sets forth critical information about an offering for potential private investors.

Registration Statement
Legal document filed with the SEC to register securities for public offering.

Related Party Transaction
An interaction between two parties, one of whom can exercise control or significant influence over the operating policies of the other. A special relationship may exist, e.g. a corporation and a major shareholder.

Selling Memorandum
Document that disseminates information to potential buyers during an auction.

Shareholder Agreement
Agreement that sets the terms by which shareholders deal with each other.

Sole Proprietorship
A business owned by a single individual.

Sub-Chapter S Corporation
A business that has the limited-liability attributes of a corporation but taxation, is treated as a partnership.

Term Sheet
Document that outlines the tenets of a deal and serves as the basis for its legal drafting.

Termination Fee
Penalty paid to the acquiror if the target backs out of the deal. See Breakup Fee.

Trademarks
Protected word, name, symbol, or device or combination thereof used by a company to identify and distinguish its goods from competitors. Carries a term of 10 years, renewable upon expiration.

Wealth Replacement Trust
Trust that owns a life insurance policy payable upon death to the trust to received by the beneficiary.

Part II

Listing of Terms
by Category

Alphabetical Listing of All Terms

2/20 Fee Model
An investment fund where investors pay a 2% management fee plus 20% carried interest (aka incentive fee).

7(a) Loan Guaranty Program
SBA program that provides loan guarantees to small businesses unable to secure financing on reasonable terms through normal lending channels. Maximum loan is $5 million and loan term is 25 years for real estate, 10 years for equipment and 7 years for working capital. 7(a) loans are fully amortized.

Acceleration Clause
A legal clause stating that the entire outstanding balance of a loan becomes payable immediately if a certain event occurs.

Accelerator
An accelerator is similar to an incubator, in that accelerators provide infrastructure and mentoring, but they are typically profit-driven. Participants have a limited time in the incubator (often 3 months) with the goal of Series A funding at the end. The accelerator generally takes some equity in each startup.

Accredited Investor
Investors who are considered by the SEC to be wealthy enough to afford to lose their investment in a worse case scenario. A single person is an accredited investor if he/she has $200,000 in annual income or a net worth of more than $1 million (excluding residence).

Accretive
Growth by gradual addition. In finance, an action is accretive if it adds to earnings per share.

Accrual Basis
Revenues and expenses are recognized in the period in which they are incurred rather than the period that they are received or paid.

Acquiree
The firm being purchased in an acquisition. See Target.

Acquirer
A firm or individual that is purchasing an equity interest in another company.

Acquisition of Assets
A merger or consolidation in which an acquirer purchases the selling firm's assets without getting any ownership of the company itself.

Acquisition of Stock
A merger or consolidation in which an acquirer purchases the acquirer's stock.

Add-On Acquisition
A horizontal purchase of similar company that increases the size of or compliments the platform company.

Adjustable Rate
Preferred stock whose dividends are reset quarterly at a predetermined spread. Can also refer to a loan with an interest rate that floats at a pre-determined margin or spread above a stated index (such as LIBOR).

Adjusted Equity
Difference between the market value of a company's assets and liabilities.

Adjusted Indicated Value
Value conclusion after any discounts or premiums are applied.

Advance Rates
The ratio relationship between the amount of money a lender extends and the value of the pledged collateral.

Affirmative Covenant
A covenant that requires the borrower to take a particular action. The borrower will be in breach unless that action is taken.

Agency Theory
The analysis of potential conflicts in principal-agent relationships, wherein one person, an agent, acts on behalf of another person, a principal.

Agent
The decision-maker in a principal-agent relationship. The agent represents the interests of the principal.

Aging Schedule
A table of accounts receivable broken down into age categories (such as 0-30 days, 30-60 days, and 60-90 days), which is used to see whether customer payments are keeping close to schedule.

AICPA
American Institute of Certified Public Accountants. The world's largest association of accountants, setting ethical standards, lobbying and providing the CPA exam.

Air-Ball
The portion of an asset-based loan that is not covered by the collateral.

All-in Cost
Total costs of a specific capital type, explicit (such as required return) and implicit (fees and other charges).

Allocation
Market process of rationing resources.

Alternative Investment
Investments other than cash or publicly traded stocks and bonds. Generally illiquid and require the investor to be an accredited investor. Can include real estate (and other real assets), hedge funds, angel investments, venture capital, private equity, and private debt.

American Stock Exchange (AMEX)
The third-largest stock exchange in the United States. It trades mostly in small-to-medium-sized companies. It is owned by the New York Stock Exchange (NYSE).

Amortization
The process of spreading the cost of an intangible asset over the expected useful life of the asset, or the repayment of the principal of a loan by installments.

Angel Investor
Wealthy investor that participates in high-risk deals with early stage companies.

Annual Exclusion Gifts
Gifts of up to $11,000 to an unlimited number of recipients that do not incur taxes.

Anti-Assignment Provision
A clause in a contract that prevents the contract from being sold or assigned to a third-party without the consent of all parties. Most relevant in asset sales, where all relevant contracts with vendors and customers must be individually renegotiated.

Anti-Dilution Rights
Protects an investor's shares in a company from being diluted if the company issues more stock.

Appraisal
An estimate of the value of a company. See Valuation.

Appraisal Remedy
Dissenter's rights statutes that serve to protect the minority, typically through the purchase of their stock at fair value.

Appraisal Standards
Standards that provide structure for the practice of valuation.

Arbitrage
A technique employed to profit from buying or selling the same security in different market places, thus making money from the disparity in market prices.

Arbitration
Process in which both sides of a deadlock present their case to a third party, who makes a binding ruling that both parties have previously committed to abide.

Armenian Handshake
Buy/Sell provision to protect minority owners. An owner cannot accept compensation from the company without sharing or getting consent from the other owners.

Arm's Length Price
The price at which a willing buyer and a willing unrelated seller would freely agree to transact.

Articles of Incorporation
Legal document establishing a corporation and its structure and purpose.

ASA
Accredited Senior Appraiser.

Asset
Any item that has tangible value and can be sold or exchanged for something else that possesses value.

Asset Approach
Method of valuation that uses the underlying assets and net liabilities of a business to derive a value.

Asset-Based Lending (ABL)
Debt that is secured by assets such as inventory, accounts receivable, real estate, etc.

Asset-Light
Refers to a business that is quickly scalable because of an exceptionally high fixed asset turnover ratio. These businesses typically have a high ROIC relative to other firms in their industry.

Asymmetric Information
Information known to some people but not to other people.

Auction Markets
Markets in which the prevailing price is determined through the free interaction of prospective buyers and sellers, as on the floor of the stock exchange.

Audit Fee
Fee charged by a lender for monitoring the borrower's collateral position and financial statements.

Audited Statements
Reports in which a public accountant has verified the accuracy of transaction recording and preparation methodology.

Balance Sheet
A financial statement that shows the assets, liabilities, and owners' equity of an entity at a particular date.

Balance Sheet Leverage Ratio
A standard measure of company leverage. Defined as Debt divided by Equity.

Balloon Payment
The balance, or final payment after monthly payments of principal and interest are paid on a loan.

Bank Lessors
When a bank provides the equipment lease, rather than a finance company or the equipment vendor.

Bankruptcy
State of being insolvent and thus unable to pay debts.

Bargain-Purchase-Price-Option
Gives the lessee the options to purchases the asset at a price below fair market value when the lease expires.

Basel III
An international regulatory scheme for banks related to stress testing, capitalization, and liquidity risk.

Basis Point
One hundredth of a percentage point.

Before and After Method
Method of valuation that compares the revenues and profits before and after the business interruption.

Best-Efforts Sale
The underwriting firm agrees to sell as much of the offering as possible and return any unsold shares to the issuer.

Beta
A measure of systematic risk of a security; the tendency of a security's returns to correlate with swings in the broad market.

BIMBO
Buy/In Management Buyout. Transaction in which business is bought out by a management team comprised of existing and incoming management.

BIO
Institutional buyout where an equity sponsor introduces new management.

Bizcomps
Database published semi-annually chronicling numerous transactions in different regions, each with approximately 20 data points of information with which to use in valuations under $5 million.

Black-Scholes
A model for pricing call options that uses the stock price, the exercise price, the risk-free interest rate, the time to expiration, and the standard deviation of the historical return of the underlying stock.

Block Voting
A group of shareholders banding together to vote their shares into a single block.

Blockage Discount
An amount or percentage deducted from the current market price of a publicly traded security to reflect the decrease in the per share value of a block of those securities that is of a size that could not be sold in a reasonable period of time given normal trading volume.

Blocked Account
Account controlled by the lender while payments are remitted during a clearance period.

Blue Sky Laws
Securities laws particular to the individual states.

Boilerplate
Standard terms and conditions. Don't accept these at face value. Hire a securities attorney to review.

Bolt-On Acquisition
A horizontal acquisition that is done primarily to increase the size (revenue) of the platform company.

Bond
A debt instrument which pays back cash to the holder at regular frequencies. The payment is normally a fixed percentage, known as a coupon. At maturity, the face value of the bond is paid.

Book Value
For valuation purposes, equals total assets minus intangible assets and liabilities from the balance sheet.

Borrowing Base
The amount that can be borrowed at a given time. Found by applying advance rates against eligible assets.

Borrowing Base Certificate
Report prepared by a borrower that shows the amount that can be borrowed at a given time.

Brand Equity
The monetary value of having a well-known brand.

Break-Even Point
The point at which revenues and costs are equal; a combination of sales and costs that will yield a no profit/no loss operation.

Breakup Fee
Penalty paid to the acquiror if the target backs out of the deal. See Termination Fee.

Bridge Financing
Interim financing (often high interest debt) of one sort or another used to solidify a position until more permanent financing is arranged.

Build-Up Method
Used by professional appraisers to calculate a discount rate. Generally starts with the risk-free rate and then premiums are added to it to arrive at an overall cost of capital.

Bulletin Board
Electronic quotation system that displays real-time quotes, last sale prices, and volume information for many over the counter stocks.

Burn-Out Round
This is a venture capital funding round for a company that is not doing well, so the share price is very low (a down round) which means that the new infusion of capital results in a high level of dilution of the stakes of the investors in prior rounds. Also known as wash-out round or a cram-down round.

Business & Industry Loans
Loans provided to rural companies with stipulation that a job must be created or retained for each $40,000 loaned.

Business Bank
A financial institution that provides business loans generally between $1MM and $3MM.

Business Broker
One who works with buyers or sellers of small businesses to help them with their transaction.

Business Cycle
Ongoing process of booms and busts in the life of a business or the economy.

Business Development Company (BDC)
A Venture Capital firm that is publicly traded, thus allowing retail investors to invest in this asset class.

Business Enterprise
A commercial, industrial, service, or investment entity, or a combination thereof, pursuing economic activity.

Business Interruption
External event that hurts the prospective earnings of a company by impeding its operations.

Business Transfer
The spectrum of possibilities, from transferring assets of a company to transferring partial or full enterprise stock interests.

Business Valuation
The act or process of determining the value of a business enterprise or ownership interest therein.

Buy and Build
Method of consolidation that uses private equity and debt for the initial acquisition of the platform company, then for the additional bolt-on acquisitions.

Buy/Sell Agreement
A binding contract between the various owners of a business that controls when an owner can sell his interest, to whom and for how much.

Buyout
Purchase of a controlling interest (or percent of shares) of a company's stock. A leveraged buy-out is done with borrowed money.

Call for Offers
Made by the intermediary of a private auction after buyer visits to gain a better perspective of the potential suitors.

Call Option
An option contract that gives its holder the right (but not the obligation) to purchase a specified number of shares of the underlying stock at the given strike price, on or before the expiration date of the contract.

Call Protection
This is a prepayment penalty that prevents the lender from losing profit on a loan if the borrower repays early.

Cap
An upper limit on the interest rate on a floating-rate note.

Capital
Long-term funds invested in a firm. Consists of equity and long-term debt. Liabilities maturing in less than one year are considered working capital, not capital.

Capital Asset
A long-term asset that is not purchased or sold in the normal course of business. Generally, it includes fixed assets, e.g., land, buildings, furniture, equipment, fixtures and furniture.

Capital Asset Pricing Model (CAPM)
An economic theory that describes the relationship between risk and expected return, and serves as a model for the pricing of risky securities.

Capital Budget
A firm's set of planned capital expenditures.

Capital Efficiency
Maximizing returns while employing the least amount of capital possible. Often measured by Return on Capital Employed (ROCE).

Capital Employed
Total liabilities less non-interest bearing liabilities.

Capital Expenditure
CAPEX is the amount used during a particular period to acquire or improve long-term assets such as property, plant, or equipment.

Capital Gain or Loss
The difference between the market and book value of a capital asset at the time of transaction.

Capital Lease
A lease obligation that has to be capitalized on the balance sheet.

Capital Structure
The mix of debt and equity financing in a business.

Capital Types
The six broad categories of capital available in the private capital markets. They include bank lending, equipment leasing, asset based lending, factoring, mezzanine debt, and private equity.

Capitalization
The process of forming capital structure through risk and return assessments or the conversion of a benefit stream to a present value.

Capitalization Rate
Any divisor used to convert a benefit stream into value.

Capitalize
To convert a benefit stream into a value.

CAPLine Program
Umbrella program under which the SBA helps small businesses meet their short-term and cyclical working capital needs.

Caps and Baskets
Terms included in the sale agreement. Caps limit the idemnification for the buyer if the seller makes a misrepresentation. Baskets are a monetary hurdle that idemnification claims must exceed before they are payable.

Captive Lessors
Subsidiaries of manufacturers that provide financing to customers in the form of an equipment lease.

Carried Interest
A percentage of an investment fund's capital gains that is paid to the fund's general partner. See incentive fee.

Cash Burn Rate
The monthly rate of cash loss in a business.

Cash Flow
Cash that is generated over a period of time by an asset, group of assets, or business enterprise.

Cash Flow Leverage Ratio
A measure often used to determine probablility of default. Defined as (Debt / EBITDA).

Cash Flow Loan
A loan where repayment probability is measured based on the cash flow of the borrower.

Catch-Up
An alternative investment fund fee structure where there is an overall incentive fee even when there is a hurdle rate in place. Thus, as soon as the hurdle rate is satisfied, the fund enters a "catch-up" phase, where all additional gains to go the general partner until the point is reached where the overall incentive fee percentage has been paid. After that, gains are split between the general partner and limited partners according to the normal schedule.

Certified Development Company 504 Program
SBA program that provides growing businesses with long-term fixed-rate financing for major fixed assets, such as land and buildings.

Change in Control Provision
Protects an employee from adverse effects if the ownership of the company changes.

Channel Expansion
Growing sales through the exploitation of new distribution approaches.

Chapter 11
Voluntary bankruptcy filing by the debtor.

Chapter 7
Involuntary liquidation forced by creditor(s).

Charitable Lead Annuity Trust
Trust that distributes a certain amount to a beneficiary at least annually for a term of years.

Charitable Lead Trust
Irrevocable trust that income to a charity for a specified period of time. Income interest to the charity must be either annuity interest or unitrust interest.

Charitable Lead Unitrust
Trust that distributes a fixed percentage of the net fair market value of its assets valued annually.

Charitable Remainder Annuity Trust
CRT that pays a fixed dollar amount or a fixed percentage of the initial fair market value of the CRT assets.

Charitable Remainder Trust
Irrevocable trust in which one or more individuals are paid income until the grantor's death, at which time the balance becomes tax free and is passed on to a designated charity.

Charitable Remainder Unitrust
Trust that pays a fixed percentage of the CRT assets valued annually.

Chart of Accounts
A list of ledger account names and associated numbers arranged in the order in which they normally appear in the financial statements.

Class of Shares
Shares of varying rights or powers that are issued by the same company (ex. Class A, Class B).

Clawback
A provision in an alternative investment fund fee structure where the general partner must refund a portion of incentive fees paid on early harvesting activities if later lower fund performance doesn't justify those incentive fees overall.

Clearance Period
See Float Days

Closing Fee
A fee charged by the lender at closing to cover such items as the funding fee, processing fees, underwriter's fee, etc.

Co-Investment
An opportunity offered to a limited partner to make a direct investment (outside of the fund) to a fund's portfolio company.

Collateral
Assets that secure a loan or other debt.

Collateral Monitoring
Process of ensuring that the assets that the borrower provided as collateral are maintained.

Collateral Value
The value of a business interest for secured lending purposes.

Commercial Bank
A financial institution that provides business loans between $3MM and $50MM.

Commission
Fee to the factor that covers the credit process that a client wishes the factor to perform.

Commitment Fee
A fee paid to a commercial bank in return for its legal commitment to lend funds that have not yet been advanced. It the loan happens, it becomes the origination fee.

Committed Capital
The amount that has been pledged to an investment fund by investors, but not yet paid to the fund.

Common Stock
The most frequently issued class of stock; usually it provides a voting right but is secondary to preferred stock in dividend and liquidation rights.

Community Bank
A financial institution that provides business loans generally less than $1MM.

Company-Specific Risk
The portion of total risk specific to an individual security that can be avoided through diversification. See Idiosyncratic Risk or Unsystematic Risk

Compensating Balance
An excess balance that is left in a bank to provide indirect compensation for loans extended or services provided.

Compound Annual Growth Rate (CAGR)
The year over year growth rate applied to an investment or other part of a company.

Compound Interest
Interest calculated from the total of original principal plus accrued interest.

Compounded Rate of Return
The rate of return on an investment where reinvestment of the cash flows increases the yield.

Compounding
The process of accumulating the time value of money forward in time.

Confidentiality Agreement
Nondisclosure agreement between buyer and seller.

Consolidation
A period where there is intensive merger activity within an industry resulting in a measurably reduced number of firms in that industry.

Consolidation
The initial acquisition of one or more platform companies, followed by the purchase of add-on acquisitions.

Contingent Liability
A liability that is dependent upon uncertain events that may occur in the future.

Contribution to Profits Method
Method of deriving amount of Key Person Insurance that multiplies the excess profit attributed to that employee by the number of years it will take to train someone to fill the vacant position.

Control
The power to direct the management and policies of a business enterprise.

Control Buyout
A purchase of equity that results in the acquirer getting a controlling majority of the company's shares.

Control Premium
An amount by which the pro rata value of a controlling interest exceeds the pro rata value of a noncontrolling interest in a business enterprise that reflects the power of control.

Control Value
Ownership interest of 51%-100% in the company.

Conversion Rights
Provisions set forth in the term sheet regarding the preferred stock conversion ratio and whether or not the ratio is fluctuating.

Convertible Debt
A debt instrument that can be exercised into the equity security of the debtor in accordance with the conditions set forth in the debt instrument.

Convertible Preferred Stock
Preferred stock that can be converted into common stock at the option of the holder.

Copyright
A form of legal protection used to safeguard original literary works, performing arts, sound recordings, visual arts, original software code and renewals. Protected for the life of the author plus 70 years.

Corporate Acquisition
The acquisition of one firm by another firm.

Corporate Bank
A financial institution that provides business loans generally more than $50MM.

Corporate Finance
The study of the manner in which companies make investment and financing decisions.

Correlation Coefficient
A standardized statistical measure of the dependence of two random variables, defined as the covariance divided by the standard deviations of two variables.

Cost Approach
Measures future benefits of ownership and amount of money necessary to replace its future service capabilities.

Cost of Capital
The expected rate of return that a market requires in order to attract funds to a particular investment.

Cost of Equity
The expected rate of return that an Individual investor requires in order to attract funds to a particular investment.

Cost of Goods Sold (COGS)
A figure representing the cost of buying raw materials and producing finished goods.

Cost of Replacement Method
Method of deriving amount of Key Person Insurance that calculates the direct costs required to interview, hire, and train a replacement, as well as the opportunity costs incurred due to the loss of the key employee.

Cost Savings Synergy
Synergy that results from expenses that are no longer needed when business functions are consolidated.

Could-Be-Public Companies
Private companies with similar characteristics to those of public companies.

Coupon
Interest payment on debt.

Covenants
Rules attached to a loan agreement that govern what the borrower can and cannot do during the loan term. Maintaining certain financial statement ratios is common.

Cram-Down Round
This is a venture capital funding round for a company that is not doing well, so the share price is very low (a down round) which means that the new infusion of capital results in a high level of dilution of the stakes of the investors in prior rounds. Also known as burn-out round or a wash-out round.

Credit Box
The qualification boundaries that must be met in order to qualify for a particular source of capital.

Credit Scoring
An analytical process designed to predict whether loan application would live up to their debt obligations.

Creditor
Lender of money.

Cross-Purchase Agreements
Buy/Sell agreement in which one or more other parties buys a business interest from an exiting party.

Crowdfunding
Raising money online in small amounts from many people (often unsophisticated). There are three categories of crowdfunding: Donation-Based Crowdfunding, Debt-Based Crowdfunding, and Equity-Based Crowdfunding.

Culture
The behaviors and values of a company that make it unique. Incompatible cultures are a common cause of integration problems with mergers.

Cumulative Preferred Stock
Preferred stock whose dividends accrue, should the issuer not make timely dividend payments.

Cure Period
A period of time specified in the loan agreement within which the borrower has to mend any violations of the loan covenant.

Current Assets
Those assets of a company that are reasonably expected to be realized in cash, or sold, or consumed during the normal operating cycle of the business (usually one year).

Current Liabilities
Liabilities that are due within the next year.

Current Maturities of Long-Term Debt
That portion of long term obligations, which is due within the next fiscal year.

Current Ratio
A measure of the liquidity of a business. Current assets divided by current liabilities.

Data Room
Area containing mass amounts of information regarding the subject of an auction.

Deal Sourcing
The process of finding acquisition target candidates in M&A and private equity.

Debt Capacity
Ability to borrow. The amount a firm can borrow up to the point where the firm value no longer increases.

Debt Service
Interest payment plus repayments of principal to creditors, that is, retirement of debt.

Debt to Equity
Measures the risk of the firm's capital structure in terms of amounts of capital contributed by creditors and that contributed by owners.

Debt-Based Crowdfunding
Crowdfunding where the public lends the borrower small amounts of money, adding up to the amount desired. Also called social lending or peer-to-peer lending. Examples are Prosper.com and LendingClub.

Debtor
1) In lending, it is the borrower. 2) In factoring, it is the entity that generates the receivable.

Default
The failure to make a payment on either the interest or principle of a debt or loan.

Default Interest Rates
Percentage increase over that of the agreed upon interest rate for violations of the loan agreement.

Default Risk
The risk that a company will be unable to pay the principal or contractual interest on its debt obligations.

Deferred Interest Balloon
Structure that defers a stated amount of interest into the future, at which point it is due in full.

Deleveraging Transaction
Any transaction that reduces a firm's debt. Commonly refers to conversion of convertible debt into stock.

Demand Loan Payment
The lender can call (cancel and demand full repayment) at any time.

Depreciation
A non-cash charge that reduces the accounting value of fixed assets due to wear, age or obsolescence.

Depreciation Tax Shield
The value of the tax write-off on depreciation of plant and equipment.

Derivative
Transaction or contract whose value depends on that of underlying assets.

Design Patent
Protects the original appearance of an article of manufacture, not its structural features. Carries a term of 14 years.

Detachable Warrant
Warrant that may be sold separately from the security with which it was originally issued.

Dilution
In asset based lending, percentage of the total invoices uncollected. Regarding equity, a watering down in the ownership stake, usually as a result of the sale of additional shares.

Dilutive
In finance, an action is dilutive if it results in decreased earnings per share.

Direct Public Offering
Do-It-Yourself IPO where the registration of the securities with the regulators is accomplished using simplified forms and procedures, such as the SCOR offering.

Direct Valuation
Value is determined by direct reference to actual comparable data.

Discount
A reduction in value or the act of reducing value. In finance refers to calculating the present value of a future cash flow using a discount rate (cost of capital). Discounting is the opposite of compounding.

Discount Fee
Factoring charge that involves two costs: a commission charge, and an interest rate for the cash advances.

Discount Rate
The expected rates of return that investors require in order to attract funds to a particular investment. See Cost of Capital.

Discounted Cash Flow (DCF)
Finding the present value of an opportunity by calculating the sum of discounted expected future cash flows.

Discretionary Earnings
The amount of a company's income available for spending after the essentials have been met.

Dissent
Action taken by minority shareholders who believe the majority has taken corporate actions that negatively affect them.

Dividend
A dividend is a portion of a company's earnings that is paid out to shareholders on a quarterly or annual basis.

Division
A self-sufficient unit within a company.

Dodd-Frank
Refers to The Dodd-Frank Wall Street Reform and Consumer Protection Act, passed in 2010. Implemented additional monitoring for financial institutions deemed "too big to fail" and imposed additional restrictions on lending to consumers. Also imposed the Volcker Rule to limit speculative trading by banks.

Donation-Based Crowdfunding
Crowdfunding the relies on donations from the public, often with a promise of a sample of the product when completed. Examples include IndieGoGo and Kickstarter.

Done Deals
Database collected from all SEC filings of acquisition transactions.

Donor
Individual who donates property to another through a trust. Also called a grantor.

Down Round
A series of venture funding where the share price is lower than the previous round of funding. This is bad for previous investors because it is highly dilutive.

Drag Along Rights
Entitlement of the majority stakeholder to force a minority stakeholder to join a transaction where it is selling its stake.

Dry Powder
Metaphorically refers to dry gunpowder, meaning that the possessor of dry powder has the ability to continue to fight. In finance, this means that the investor still has a cash reserve with which to make additional investments.

Due Diligence
The discovery and examination period after execution of a letter of intent.

Dutch Auction
An auction where the bidding starts at a high price and then the auctioneer incrementally lowers the price until it reaches a point where the entire offering is sold.

Early Equity Value
The value of a business interest as a startup, often prior to profit or even revenue.

Early Stage
An enterprise that have been operational less than three years, may have revenue, unlikely to be profitable.

Earning Capacity
The future profit picture of a firm.

Earnings Before Interest and Taxes (EBIT)
The figure for operating income after depreciation but without allowing for debt service or what is owed to the government for taxes.

Earnings Before Interest, Taxes, Depreciation and Amor
Earnings before interest, taxes, depreciation, and amortization.

Earn-Out
Method for triggering changes in the purchase price based on future performance of the subject company. The seller "earns" a portion of the purchase price by the company meeting ageed-upon future performance milestones.

EBITDAR
Earnings before interest, taxes, depreciation, amortization and rent.

Economic Benefit Stream
This benefit stream is 'economic' because it is either derived by recasting financial statements or determined on a pro forma basis. Streams may be comprised of earnings, cash flow, and/or distributions.

Economic Life
The period of time over which property may generate economic benefits. Often the amount of time a piece of equipment is expected to last.

Economic Value
Measurement of generating a return in excess of the corresponding cost of capital.

Economies of Scale
Efficiencies created by increasing the size of an enterprise when there are high fixed costs versus variable costs. The increased output spreads the fixed costs more thinly across the output units thereby increasing margin.

EDGAR
The Securities & Exchange Commission Electronic Data Gathering and Retrieval to transmit company documents such as 10-Ks, 10-Qs, quarterly reports, and other SEC filings, to investors.

Effective Interest Rate
Interest rate after applying the "terms cost".

Efficient Market
A market in which new information is available to all parties and is very quickly reflected accurately in asset prices.

Efficient Portfolio
A portfolio that provides the greatest expected return for a given level of risk, or equivalently, the lowest risk for a given expected return.

Eligible Assets
Assets that qualify for advances on an asset based loan.

Emerging Markets
The financial markets of developing economies.

Employee Stock Ownership Plan (ESOP)
A company contributes to a trust fund that buys stock on behalf of employees.

Employment Agreement
Agreement that sets the terms for continued employment upon the closing of a buyout.

Engineered Intra-Transfers
Custom-tailored solutions designed to transfer all or part of the business internally.

Enterprise
See Business Enterprise.

Enterprise Value
Value of 100% of the ownership.

Entity
In business it is a separate or self-contained body that provides goods or services.

Equipment Leasing
Commercial finance provider that provide lease funding for equipment used in the operations of a business.

Equity Kicker
Stock options or warrants to purchase stock given by a company to a lender or other party as an inducement to lend money or provide some other value.

Equity Mezzanine Capital
Subordinated debt that relies on coupon plus warrants for its return.

Equity Net Cash Flows
Those cash flows available to pay out to equity holders (in the form of dividends) after funding operations of the business enterprise, making necessary capital investments, and reflecting increases or decreases in debt financing. See Cash Flow to Equity.

Equity Penalties
Agreements that increase an investor's percentage of ownership upon the occurrence of a certain event.

Equity Recapitalization
A private equity technique where the company sells a portion of the company to a PEG (using a mix of debt and equity) allowing the founder to have a partial liquidity event. The founder retains some ownership and stays involved for a number of additional years until a full buyout occurs, giving the founder a second bite at the apple.

Equity Risk Premium
The amount that investors are compensated for assuming nondiversifiable equity risk.

Equity Split
Percentage of the company that each investor owns.

Equity Sponsor
Private equity provider that finances a buyout for a management team.

Equity Sponsored Buyout
A management team partners with an equity sponsor (provider) to perform a buyout.

Equity Upside
When a capital provider experiences a gain when the company succeeds.

Equity-Based Crowdfunding
Crowdfunding where investors get equity shares of the startups.
Under Regulation A+ even non-accredited investors can invest.

ERISA
Employee Retirement Income Security Act of 1974.

ESOP Tax Deferral
The ability to sell stock to a Trust and defer or permanently avoid
taxation on any gain resulting from the sale.

Estate
All the assets a person possesses at the time of death, including
securities, real estate, interest in business, physical possessions, and
cash.

Estate Freeze
The seller freezes the value of the business at the date of transfer,
and the grantee benefits from the appreciation of the stock
thereafter.

Estate Tax
A tax imposed by a state or the federal government on assets left to
heirs in a will.

Eurobond
A bond that is (1) underwritten by an international syndicate, (2)
offered at issuance simultaneously to investors in a number of
countries, and (3) issued outside the jurisdiction of any single
country.

Eurodollar
U.S. dollars deposited in foreign banks or foreign branches of U.S.
banks.

Excess Earnings
That amount of anticipated benefits that exceeds a fair rate of return on the value of a selected asset base (often net tangible assets) used to generate those anticipated benefits.

Exchange
The venue or trading activity between market participants.

Exchangeable
Preferred stock that can be exchanged into a debt security, normally at the election of the issuer.

Exercise
To implement the right of the holder of an option to buy or sell the underlying security.

Exercise Date
Date upon which the option or warrant can be purchased or sold.

Exercise Price
Price at which the stock underlying a call or put option can be purchased (call) or sold (put) over the specified period. Also called strike price.

Exit
An event for a private business that allows equity investors to sell their shares, such as an LBO or an acquisition.

Exit Strategy
Investor insistence on certain rights so they may realize the value of their investment if they see fit to exit.

Expansion Stage
An enterprise that in experiencing rapid growth, may or may not be profitable.

Expected Future Cash Flows
Projected future cash flows associated with an asset of decision.

Expected Rate of Return
The rate of return expected on an investment by the capital provider.

Expiration
The date and time after which the option may no longer be exercised.

Explicit Weighting
The assignment of percentage weights to different methods of valuation for stated reasons.

Export Working Capital Program
SBA program designed to provide short-term working capital to exporters.

Export-Import Bank
This bank supports the financing of U.S. goods and services.

Expression of Interest
Document signed by the top prospects in an auction that narrows attention to the best suitors.

Face Value
The amount an issuer agrees to pay upon maturity.

Facility Amount
Total credit facility in place.

Factoring
The process of purchasing accounts receivable at a discount.

Fair Market Value
The price at which the property would change hands between a willing buyer and a willing seller when the buyer is not under any compulsion to buy and the seller is not under any compulsion to sell, and both parties having reasonable knowledge of relevant

Fair Valuation Date
Date before the effectuation of the corporate action to which the dissenter objects.

Fair Value
The value of the shares immediately before a corporate action to which the dissenter objects, excluding any appreciation or depreciation in anticipation of the corporate action unless exclusion would be inequitable.

Fair Value (FASB definition)
The amount at which an asset (or liability) could be bought (or incurred) or sold (or settled) in a current transaction between willing parties, that is, other than in a forced or liquidation sale.

Family Limited Partnership
Limited partnership in which only family members are included as partners.

Family Office
An entity whose sole activity is managing the trusts and investments of a single family.

FASB
Financial Accounting Standards Board

Features
Characteristics of a particular security such as whether or not it is convertible, redeemable, exchangeable, etc.

Federal Reserve System
The central bank of the U.S., established in 1913, and governed by the Federal Reserve Board located in Washington, D.C.

Fee Clock
Timeframe for charges owed to the factor once it receives the invoice from the client.

Fiduciary
A person, company, or association who is responsible for investing the assets of the beneficiary in a prudent manner.

Finance
A discipline concerned with determining value and making decisions. The finance function allocates resources, which includes acquiring, investing, and managing resources.

Finance Lease
Noncancellable lease which requires the lessee to remit payments of lease rentals that total the cost of the asset plus the lessor's required profit.

Financial Accounting Standards Board (FASB)
An accounting oversight committee that sets accounting standards for U.S. firms.

Financial Barn Raising
The act of soliciting a placement by leveraging community relationships.

Financial Boundaries
Financial statement ratios that a bank requires from a borrower over the term of the loan. See covenants.

Financial Buyer
A buyer that is intending to buy the company, hold for a period of time, then sell. The alternative is a strategic buyer that wants to integrate the target company into their long-term strategy.

Financial Control Premium
Control value of an enterprise based on financial returns.

Financial Engineer
One who combines or divides existing financial methods or instruments to create new financial products or services.

Financial Intermediaries
Brokers or arrangers of financial transactions, or institutions (such as banks) that take deposits from one party and then make loans to other parties.

Financial Sponsor
The financial sponsor in a deal is typically the private equity firm that manages a leveraged buyout.

Fiscal Policy
Government policy regarding taxation and spending. Fiscal policy is made by Congress and Administration.

Fiscal Year
The declared accounting year for a company.

Five Cs of Credit
Five characteristics that are used to form a judgement about a customer's creditworthiness: character, capacity, capital, collateral, and conditions.

Fixed Asset
A long-term tangible asset that is not expected to be converted into cash in the current or upcoming fiscal year.

Fixed Asset Turnover Ratio
Ratio of net sales to fixed assets. A company that has a high fixed asset turnover ratio is considered to be "asset-light" and thus more scalable.

Fixed Charge
Current fixed obligations on a cash basis.

Fixed Charge Coverage Ratio (FCC)
A measure often used to determine probablility of default. Defined as (EBITDA. - CAPEX - Taxes) / (Interest + Principal).

Fixed Expenses
Expenses that remain the same regardless of production or sales volume in contrasts with Variable Expenses.

Fixed Interest Rate
The fixed percentage paid for borrowing money.

Float
1. The time between the deposit of checks in a bank and when the amount is truly accessible; 2. The amount of funds represented by checks that have been written but not yet presented for payment. Some entries will 'play the float' by writing checks altho

Float Days
The period of time payments are remitted to a lender until the funds are actually credited by the lender through automated clearinghouse procedures. Also known as a Clearance Period.

Floating Rate Note
Security whose coupon rate fluctuates in line with a benchmark interest rate.

Flotation Costs
The total costs of issuing and selling a public security.

Forced Liquidation Value
Estimated gross amount of money that could be realized from sale in public auction, or negotiated liquidation sale with seller having a sense of immediacy.

Forward Rate Lock
Allows a client to "lock in" a certain interest rate for settlement on a specified date in the future.

Free Cash Flow
Net income plus non-cash charges to income, specifically depreciation and amortization less capital expenditures, to sustain the basic business.

Free Cash Flow to Equity
Those cash flows available to pay out to equity holders (in the form of dividends) after funding operations of the business enterprise, making necessary capital investments, and reflecting increases or decreases in debt financing. See Equity Net Cash Flow.

Function
The specific use of an appraisal, which leads directly to the choice of appropriate methods to employ.

Fund Lifetime
An investment fund typically has a finite life, which is often ten years (plus two optional one-year extensions at the discretion of the general partner).

Funded Amount
Credit used at a particular time.

Funded Debt
Debt maturing after more than one year.

Fundless Sponsor
A private equity investor that invests their own funds directly rather than as a limited partner in an investment fund. (a.k.a Independent Sponsor).

Fundraising
The early phase of an alternative investment fund where the general partner seeks limited partner investors to committed capital. The manager of the fund typical contributes up to 5% of the raise.

Future
Agreement between two parties to perform a trade in the future at a fixed price.

Future Value
The amount of money that an investment made today (the present value) will grow to by some future date. Since money has time value, we naturally expect the future value to be greater than the present value. The difference between the two depends on the number of compounding periods involved and the interest rate.

Futures
A term used to designate all contracts covering the sale of financial instruments or physical commodities for future delivery on a commodity exchange.

General Ledger
The accounting records that show all the financial statement accounts of a business.

General Partner
In an FLP, usually the parents or corporation owned by the parents typically holding a nominal partnership interest.

Generally Accepted Accounting Principles (GAAP)
A technical accounting term that encompasses the conventions, rules, and procedures necessary to define accepted accounting practice at a particular time.

Generation Skipping Tax
Tax on transfers to a grandchild or more remote relative, or a non-family member, who is more than 37 1/2 years younger than the transferor.

Globalization
Tendency toward a worldwide investment environment, and the integration of national capital markets.

Going Concern
An ongoing operating business enterprise

Going Concern Assumption
Assumption that a business will remain in operation indefinitely.

Going Concern Value
The value of a business enterprise that is expected to continue to operate into the future.

Going Private
Publicly owned stock is replaced with complete equity ownership by a private group.

Going Public
Undergoing an initial public offering.

Goodwill
The intangible asset arising as a result of name, reputation, customer loyalty, location, products, and similar factors not separately identified.

Goodwill Value
The value attributable to goodwill.

Governance
The way in which major financial and legal issues of the company will be managed as presented in the term sheet.

Grant
When shares of stock are given outright, rather than just an option to buy stock at a certain price.

Grantee
The person or entity to whom property or assets are transferred. See Beneficiary.

Grantor
The person or entity who transfers property or assets.

Grantor Retained Annuity Trust
Irrevocable trust that pays an annuity to the term holder for a fixed time period.

Grantor Retained Unitrust
The grantor's retained interest is a specified percentage of the trust's fair market value each year, instead of a fixed dollar amount.

Gross Domestic Product (GDP)
The total value of goods and services produced in the national economy in a given year.

Gross Margin Enhancements
Synergy benefit that occurs when one party's gross margin is improved due to another party's efficiency in the production cycle.

Gross Profit
Net sales minus cost of sales (aka Gross Margin).

Gross Sales
The total revenue at invoice value prior to any discounts or allowances,

Growth Capital
External capital inflow to the firm that is intended for expansion of the business, rather than for working capital or refinancing purposes.

Hard Hurdle
Incentive fee doesn't start until after fund reaches hurdle rate. With catch-up, all profits go to incentive fee after hurdle rate is achieved, until overall carried interest rate to manager has been reached.

Harvest Period
In private equity, this is typically the last five years of the fund, when portfolio companies are sold.

Hedge
A term to describe protective maneuvering by an investment manager to reduce the risk of a loss from a specified event.

Hedge Fund
Historically, an alternative investment fund using publicly traded derivatives to limit downside investment risk. Now, hedge funds can generically refer to nearly any investment strategy that uses a limited partnership fund structure.

Holding Company
A company which owns or controls other companies.

Horizontal Integration
Merger or acquisition involving two or more firms in the same industry in the same position in the supply chain.

Human Capital
The combined knowledge, skill, innovativeness, and ability of the company's individual employees to meet the task at hand.

Hurdle Rate
The required return in capital budgeting. Specifically, the minimum expected IRR that a venture would require to be approved.

Hurdle Rate
The minimum return that a fund must reach before incentive fees are paid.

Hybrid Agreement
Buy/sell agreement that allows the founder first priority to buy an exiting interest with other owners or partners second in line to purchase.

Idemnification
Immunity from financial or legal liability.

Idiosyncratic Risk
The portion of total risk specific to an individual security that can be avoided through diversification. See Unsystematic Risk or Company-Specific Risk

IMAP
International Network of M&A Partners. A worldwide group of investment bankers that advise in the sale of private companies.

Impaired Goodwill
According to SFAS 142, if goodwill carried on the balance sheet is worth more than its current "fair value," the difference must be written off.

Impairment Test
Test for goodwill impairment at the reporting unit level.

Implicit Weighting
The weighting of a value conclusion based on the adjusted indicated values of various valuation methods.

Incentive Fee
A percentage of an investment fund's capital gains that is paid to the fund's general partner. See carried interest.

Income Approach
Method of valuation that ultimately converts anticipated benefits into a present value.

Income Statement
The financial statement that summarizes the revenues and expenses of a company over a specified period of time.

Incremental Business Value (IBV)
A measure of how much value that management has added to the company. IBV = Recast EBITDA - (Investment x private cost of capital).

Incubator
An organization that provides infrastructure and mentoring for startups. They are often sponsored by local governments.

Independent Lessors
General leasing companies that may be affiliated with a larger finance company.

Independent Sponsor
A private equity investor that invests their own funds directly rather than as a limited partner in an investment fund. (a.k.a Fundless Sponsor).

Indirect Valuation
Value is determined using a method that indirectly estimates value.

Industrial Revenue Bonds
Municipal bonds whose proceeds are loaned to private persons or businesses to finance capital investment projects.

Inflation
An increase in the general price level of goods and services; alternatively, a decrease in the purchasing power of the dollar or other currency.

Inflection Point
A significant change in the progress or direction of a company.

Information Asymmetry
A situation involving information that is known to some but not all participants.

Information Efficiency
The speed and accuracy with which prices reflect new information.

Information Opacity
Condition caused by private shareholders aversion, or inability, to grant potential capital providers with all pertinent information about their companies financial outlook, current operations and future prospects.

Initial Public Offering (IPO)
A company's first sale of stock to the public.

Insider
Directors, officers, and others in a corporation who know of or have access to confidential information that has not been released to the general public.

Installment Sale
The sale of an asset in exchange for a specified series of payments (the installments).

Institute of Business Appraisers (IBA)
The oldest business appraisal society in the U. S.

Institutional Investor
An entity, company, mutual fund, insurance corporation, brokerage, or other such group that invests.

Insurable Value
One of a number of appropriate values that may be used to determine the funding amount for a buy/sell agreement or the value sought for determining the necessary amount of insurance coverage or claim.

Intangible Assets
Non-physical assets (such as franchises, trademarks, patents, copyrights, goodwill, equities, mineral rights, securities, and contracts as distinguished from physical assets) that grant rights, privileges, and have economic benefits for the owner.

Intellectual Assets
Intangible assets particular to a company that add to the enterprise value.

Intellectual Capital
The sum of Human Capital and Structural Capital.

Intellectual Property
An original idea or concept of the creator that can be trademarked, patented, copyrighted, or held as a trade secret.

Intentionally Defective Grantor Trust
Trust that takes stock in exchange for a promissory note. The grantor pays estate tax on the note and accumulated interest but avoids income tax since it sees no gain or loss.

Intercreditor Agreement
An agreement between all lenders on a deal that delineates who owns what rights and when they get paid.

Interest
The price paid for the borrowing money

Interest Expense
The cost of borrowing funds in the current period.

Interest Rate
The percentage paid for borrowing money.

Interest Rate Cap
Sets a maximum boundary, or limit, on a given floating interest rate.

Interest Rate Collar
Sets a maximum and minimum boundary on a given floating interest rate.

Interest Rate Hedges
Methods by which interest rates are offset, or controlled, by the borrower for a price

Interest Tax Shield
The reductions in income taxes that result from the tax-deductibility of interest payments.

Intermediation
Assisting the exchange process in a market.

Internal Rate of Return
Discount rate at which investment has a net present value equal to zero.

Invested Capital
The amount of an investment fund's committed capital that has actually been invested by the general partner.

Invested Capital
The sum of equity and debt in a business enterprise.

Investee
Entity that receives capital.

Investment Banker
Financial intermediary who assists companies in accessing the capital markets and performs a variety of services, including aiding in the sale of securities, facilitating mergers and other corporate reorganizations.

Investment Horizon
Timeframe within which an investor will exit an investment.

Investment Period
Generally the first three to five years of a private equity or venture capital fund, when the general partner finds companies to invest in.

Investment Round
A single attempt to raise capital through the issuance of stock.

Investment Value
The value of a business interest to a particular investor.

Investor's Rights
Privileges of the investor outlined in the term sheet.

Invoice
An itemized list of goods shipped usually specifying the price and the terms of sale.

Irrevocable Life Insurance Trust
See Wealth Replacement Trust

IRS Published Interest Rate
Benchmark interest rate set forth by the IRS.

Issue
In securities, issue is stock or bonds sold by a corporation or a government; or, the selling of new securities by a corporation or government through an underwriter or private placement.

Issuer
Company offering securities.

Key Person
Important person without whom a company can expect to experience a decrease in future income.

Key Person Discount
An amount or percentage deducted from the value of an ownership interest to reflect the reduction in value resulting from the actual or potential loss of a key person in a business enterprise.

Lack of Marketability Discount
An amount or percentage deducted from the value of an ownership interest to reflect the relative absence of marketability.

Last Survivor Annuity
Private annuity whose payments continue until the death of the
last survivor.

Later Stage
Venture capital funding rounds that are after startup / Series A,
meaning Series B and beyond.

Lease Factor
A mathematical expression that describes the lease payment as a
decimal/fraction of the equipment acquisition cost.

Lehman Formula
A compensation formula originally developed by investment
bankers Lehman Brothers for investment banking services: 5% of
the first million dollars involved in the transaction for services
needed, 4% of the second million, 3% of the third million, 2% of
the fourth million, 1% of everything thereafter.

Lessee
An entity that leases an asset from another entity.

Lessor
An entity that leases an asset to another entity.

Letter of Credit
A written agreement issued by the bank and given to the seller at
the request of the buyer to pay up to a stated sum of money.

Letter of Intent
A legally nonbinding agreement that describes the important terms
of a deal.

Letter Stock
Privately placed common stock, so-called because the SEC requires
a letter from the purchaser stating that the stock is not intended
for resale.

Leverage

The use of debt to improve the financial performance of an enterprise. Can also specifically refer to an accounting ratio that measure the proportion of debt in the capital structure of a company, such as the debt/equity ratio.

Leveraged Buyout (LBO)

The use of borrowed money to finance the purchase of a firm.

Leveraged ESOP

ESOP that borrows money from a lender that is then repaid by the company through tax-deductible contributions to a Trust.

Leveraged Recapitalization

When a company takes on significant debt in order to pay dividends or repurchase stock. See Equity Recapitalization.

Levered Beta

The beta reflecting a capital structure that includes debt.

LIBOR

The London Interbank Offered Rate; the rate of interest that major international banks in London charge each other for borrowings.

Lien

A security interest in one or more assets that is granted to lenders in connection with secured debt financing.

Lifestyle Business

Firms that are not seeking value maximization as a primary objective.

Lifetime Exclusion Gifts

Gifts that may total up to $1 million over the course of one's lifetime without incurring any taxes.

Limited Liability Company (LLC)
Form of business organization in which each owner of the business is not liable for the debts of the business unless they have personally covenanted to accept such an obligation.

Limited Partner
A partner who has limited legal liability for the obligations of the partnership.

Line of Credit
An agreement whereby a financial institution promises to lend up to a certain amount without the need to file another loan application.

Liquidated Collateral
Likely cash value of collateral in liquidation.

Liquidation Preference
In the event of an IPO or acquisition, this indicates the order in which investors get paid and how much. 1x liquidation preference means the investor gets 100% of original investment back before the remaining capital gains are split among all investors.

Liquidation Value
Net amount that could be realized by selling the assets of a firm after repaying the debt. Value of a firm in dissolution.

Liquidity
The amount and ease by which an asset can be converted to cash. Frequently measure by the current ratio.

Loan Covenant
Agreements between lenders and borrowers requiring the borrowers to follow certain guidelines over the term of the loan.

Loan Guaranty
Percentage of a loan that the SBA or other government agency guarantees.

Loan-to-Value Ratio
See Advance Rates.

Lockbox
A collection and processing service provided to firms by financial institutions that collect payments from a dedicated postal box that the firm directs its customers to send payment to. Located geographically to reduce mail time.

Long-Term Liabilities
Liabilities of a business due in more than one year. An example of a long-term liability would be mortgage payable.

Lost Profits
Commercial damages due to a business interruption.

Lower Middle Market
Businesses with annual revenues between $5MM and $100MM.

M&A Intermediary
Firm that focuses on providing merger, acquisition, and divestiture services to middle market companies.

MACRS
Modified accelerated cost recovery system.

Majority Interest
An ownership interest greater than fifty percent (50%) of the voting interest in a business enterprise.

Management Buy-In
Purchase of an ownership interest by a management team not currently involved in the business.

Management Buyout
Buyout by existing management of part or all of the ownership of the company.

Management Fee
The fixed percentage fee that is paid to an investment fund's general partner regardless of performance. Can be a percentage of committed capital or invested capital.

Margin Appreciation
An increase in the gross margin of a company.

Marginal Cost of Capital
The firm's incremental cost of capital associated with its next dollar of total new financing.

Margined Collateral
The result of an advance rate applied against a qualifying asset.

Market Approach
Method of valuation that compares the subject to similar businesses, business ownership interests, securities, or intangible assets that have been sold.

Market Capitalization
The total dollar value of all outstanding shares. Computed as shares times current market price. It is a measure of corporate size.

Market Maker
Firm that stands ready to buy and sell a particular stock on a regular and continuous basis at a publicly quoted price.

Market Mechanisms
An organized set of activities that enable people to exchange or invest.

Market Penetration
The amount of revenue of a particular company as a percentage of the total theoretical size of their market.

Market Value
The highest purchase price available in the marketplace for selected assets or stock of the company.

Marketability
The ability to quickly convert property to cash at minimal cost.
See Liquidity.

Marketable Minority Interest
Minority interest assumed to be freely tradable in the marketplace.

Master Lease
An agreement that consolidates individual lease transactions into a
single leasing program.

Maturity
The date when a loan must be repaid.

Maturity Factoring
An account receivable item is purchased on the date payment is
due on the account.

Mean
The expected value of a random variable.

Median
The value of the midpoint variable when the data are arranged in
ascending or descending order.

Mediation
Process in which a mediator hears both sides of a deadlock and
rules in favor of one. Both sides must agree with the decision in
order to move forward.

Merchant Cash Advance
The purchase of a company's future credit card purchases at a
discount. Similar to factoring.

Merger
The union of two or more commercial interests or corporations.

Mezzanine Debt
Subordinated debt that provides borrowing capability beyond senior debt while minimizing the dilution associated with equity capital. Relies on the coupon for its primary source of return.

Middle Market
A segment of privately and publicly held companies whose annual sales range from $5 million to $1 billion.

Migration
Movement of customers from the commercial or corporate part of the bank to the more strictly monitored asset-based lending group.

Milestones
Included in the term sheet, they set forth certain benchmarks for the company, with corresponding staged investments.

Mini-IPO
A company that raises money under Reg A+ of Title IV of the JOBS Act. Compliance and disclosure requirements are lighter than with traditional public companies.

Minority Discount
A discount for lack of control applicable to a minority interest.

Minority Interest
An ownership interest less than fifty percent (50%) of the voting interest in a business enterprise

Model Business Corporation Act
A model act developed by the American Bar Association to help modernize and harmonize state laws governing the formation and operation of corporations.

Monetary Policy
A federal government policy pursued by the Federal Reserve to control interest rates and the money supply.

Monitoring
Surveillance of a borrower by the bank to ensure the loan is being used properly.

Monte Carlo Simulation
An analytical technique for solving a problem by performing a large number of trail runs, called simulations, and inferring a solution from the collective results of the trial runs. Method for calculating the probability distribution of possible outcomes.

Multiple Compensation Method
Method of deriving amount of Key Person Insurance that multiplies that employee's compensation by the number of years it will take to train someone to fill the vacant position.

NACVA
National Association of Certified Valuation Analysts.

NASDAQ
National Association of Securities Dealers Automated Quotations.

Negative Covenant
Agreements that restrict the actions of the corporation and ownership during the term of the loan. If the borrower takes that certain prohibited action, they will be in breach.

Negotiated Transfer
Transfer method where the parties work out a deal.

Net Asset Value
The adjustment of a company's assets and liabilities to market values.

Net Present Value (NPV)
The present value of the expected future cash flows minus the cost.

New York Stock Exchange (NYSE)
Also known as the Big Board or the Exchange. More than 2,000 common and preferred stocks are traded. The exchange is the oldest and largest in the United States. It is located on Wall Street in New York City.

Niche
A small part of a market that has potential for profitable exploitation.

No Shop
Period stipulated in a letter of intent within which the company or its agents cannot solicit other investor interest.

Non-Advocacy
Stance of indifference an appraiser must take in order to conduct a fair and unbiased appraisal.

Non-Cash Charge
A cost, such as depreciation, depletion, or amortization, that does not involve any cash outflow.

Nonmarketable Minority Interest
Minority interest for which there is no active market.

Nonmaturity Factoring
Factor purchases invoice upon shipment receipt.

Non-Operating Assets
Assets not necessary to ongoing operations of the business enterprise.

Non-Recourse Factoring
A factor has no claim against the client if the debtor defaults.

Non-Strategic Transfer
A transfer involving a buyer not strategic to the business.

Nonvoting Shares
Common shares with no voting rights.

Normalized Capital Expenditures
Expected average capital expenditures.

Offeree
Investor to whom securities are offered.

Offering Memorandum
A document that outlines the terms of securities to be offered in a private placement.

Offeror
See Issuer

One-Step Auction
Auction that concurrently encourages interest within a limited group of buyers.

Operating Expense
The amount paid for asset maintenance or the cost of doing business.

Operating Income
Revenue less cost of goods sold less operating expenses.

Operating Lease
Lease extended for small part of the useful life of the equipment. Lessor expected to return the equipment after term.

Operating Partner
A member of the management team of a private equity fund who works directly with the portfolio companies to increase value.

Operating Profit
Gross Profit minus Operating Expenses.

Opportunity Cost of Capital
Expected return that is foregone by investing in a project rather than in comparable financial securities.

Oppression
Legal term meaning the minority shareholder's reasonable expectations have not been met.

Optimal Capital Structure
The capital structure at which firm value is maximized.

Option
Gives the buyer the right, but not the obligation, to buy or sell an asset at a set price on or before a given date.

Option Price
Also called the option premium, the price paid by the buyer of the options contract for the right to buy or sell a security at a specified price in the future.

Orderly Liquidation Value
Estimated gross amount of money that could be realized from a sale, given reasonable time to find purchasers, with the seller being compelled to sell as is.

Organic Growth
Company growth fueled solely by retained earnings rather than by outside investment.

Outstanding Shares
The number of shares currently owned by all investors.

Overhead
The costs associated with providing and maintaining a manufacturing or working environment that cannot be traced directly to the production or sale of identifiable goods and services.

Oversubscribed
When during the fundraising phase of an investment fund, the fundraising goal is exceeded.

Over-the-Counter (OTC)
A computerized network (NASDAQ) through which trades of bonds, non-listed stocks, and other securities take place.

Ownership Agreements
Legal agreements that define the rights and privileges of the owners.

Pareto's Law
The 80/20 Rule that applies to innumerable situations. For example, 80% of profits come from 20% of the deals.

Pari Passu
Pari Passu translates as "without partiality" from Latin. It is used in reference to two classes of securities or obligations that have equal entitlement to payment.

Participating Preferred
Convertible preferred stock that provides the holder with extraordinary rights in the event the company is sold or liquidated.

Patent
The grant of a property right by the U.S. government to the inventor by action of the Patent and Trademark office.

Payback Period
The length of time it takes to recover the initial cost of a project, without regard to the time value of money.

Payment-In-Kind (PIK)
Debt that gives the issuer an option (during an initial period) either to make coupon payments in cash or in the form of additional bonds.

Penny Warrants
Warrant that has a nominal price to the investor.

Perfected First Lien
A first lien that is duly recorded with the cognizant governmental body so that the lender will be able to act on it should to borrower default.

Performance Ratchets
Incentive bonuses written into finance agreements that encourages management to perform.

Period of Restoration
The theoretical reasonable amount of time that it should take the insured to repair the damage of the business interruption and resume operations.

Perquisite
Personal benefits accruing to owners or employees of a business that is derived from sources other than wages.

Personal Guarantee
Collateral security over personally owned assets.

Phantom Stock
Right to a bonus based upon the performance of shares of a corporation's common stock (without actually receiving those shares) over a specified period of time.

Piggy Back Registration
When an underwriter allows existing holdings of shares in a corporation to be sold in conjunction with an offering of new shares.

Pink Sheets
Listings of price quotes for companies that trade in the over the counter market.

Pipeline
The list of potential deals that are in development but typically not yet engaged.

Platform Company
Company that forms the foundation of a business. Additional companies are acquired and added to the platform.

Point-In-Time Value
Appraised value of a private firm at a particular point-in-time.

Points
Finance charges paid by the borrower at the beginning of a loan in addition to monthly interest; each point equals one percent of the loan amount.

Poof IPO
See Roll-Up

Portfolio
A collection of investments, real and/or financial.

Portfolio Company
A company owned by a private equity fund as part of their investment portfolio.

Portfolio Discount
An amount or percentage that may be deducted from the value of a business enterprise to reflect the fact that it owns dissimilar operations or assets that may not fit well together.

Portfolio Theory
Theory holding that the risk inherent in any single asset, when held in a group of assets, is different from the inherent risk of that asset in isolation. Used to manage a collection of risky assets.

Post-Money Valuation
The "pre-money" valuation of the company plus the amount of the investment.

Pratt's Stats
Official database of the International Business Brokers Association. Covers acquisitions in the $1-30 million range and details over seventy different data fields per transaction.

Preemptive Rights
The rights of the investor to acquire new securities issued by the company to the extent necessary to maintain its percentage interest on a converted basis.

Preferences
Advantages granted to owners of preferred stock (versus common stock)

Preferred Return
The return that an investment fund must achieve before carried interest is paid to the general partner. A common level for the preferred return is around 8%. See Hurdle Rate.

Preferred Stock
A security that shows ownership in a corporation and gives the holder a claim, prior to the claim of common stockholders, on earnings and also generally on assets in the event of liquidation. Preferred stock of public companies generally does not have voting rights, whereas preferred stock in private companies often has super-voting rights.

Pre-IPO Studies
Conducted to determine a stock's marketability discount upon initial offering.

Pre-Money Valuation
Value of a company prior to accepting further investment.

Prepayment Fees
Penalties to the borrower for terminating a loan before the term expires.

Present Value
The value today of a future payment, or stream of payments, discounted at some appropriate interest rate.

Price/Earnings Ratio
Shows the "multiple" of earnings at which a public stock sells.

Prime Premium
The premium one pays for borrowing at the Prime Rate rather than LIBOR.

Prime Rate
The interest rate banks have historically charged their most creditworthy customers.

Principal
(1) The total amount of money being borrowed or lent. (2) The party affected by agent decisions in a principal-agent relationship.

Principle of Substitution
Value is determined by the cost of acquiring an equally desirable substitute.

Private Annuities
Transfer of stock in exchange for an unsecured promise to receive a stream of fixed payments for the life of the seller.

Private Auction
Selling process in which an intermediary simultaneously contacts a limited number of prospects in an attempt to confidentially maximize the selling price.

Private Capital Access Index
A quarterly index produced by Pepperdine University that measures the level to which private businesses have been able to access funding. Index values range between 0 and 100.

Private Capital Demand Index
A quarterly index produced by Pepperdine University that measures the demand for growth capital by private businesses. Index values range between 0 and 100.

Private Capital Markets
Markets where private debt and equity are raised and exchanged.

Private Corporation
A corporation that ownership is held by the private sector, i.e. individuals or companies,

Private Debt
Technically this is any borrowing done by a company that is not a public bond issue. It more typically refers to debt placed directly with investors or hedge funds.

Private Equity
Refers to the various organizations that provide equity capital to private companies.

Private Equity Group (PEG)
Typically refers to the managers of a fund that invests in the equity of private companies, especially later stage firms.

Private Guideline Search
Method that uses comparable acquisitions, analyzes them, and attempts to derive a value decision based on the information gathered.

Private Investment Banker
One that helps private companies access the private capital markets.

Private Placement
A nonpublic offering of securities exempt from full SEC registration made directly by the issuing company, but can also be made by an underwriter.

Private Placement Memorandum (PPM)
Document that sets forth critical information about an offering for potential private investors.

Private Return Expectation
The expected rate of return that the private capital markets require in order to attract funds to a particular investment. .

Pro Forma Earnings
Projected earnings.

Pro Forma Statement
A financial statement showing the forecast or projected operating results and balance sheet, as in pro forma income statements, balance sheets, and statements of cash flows.

Probability-weighted Analysis
Incorporating expectations about possible variation in the amount or timing of cash flows into an analysis.

Promissory Note
Written promise to pay.

Proportionate Interests
Notion that dissenting shareholders have the right to see their equity stake valued on a going concern basis rather than a liquidation basis.

Public Auction
Auction where confidentiality is not important and selling price is a function of a bidding war.

Public Guideline Companies
Public companies used in the valuation of a private company due to the comparative qualities between them.

Public Markets
Markets where public debt and equity are raised and exchanged.

Put Option
The right but not the obligation to sell an underlying at a particular price (strike price) on or before the expiration date of the contract.

Quiet Period
Time between the filing of a Registration Statement and its acceptance by the SEC.

Ratchets
Device to encourage management to perform against defined targets. Can also refer to mechanisms that prevent dilution of equity positions of current investors by future investors.

Rational Expectations
The idea that people rationally anticipate the future and respond to what they see ahead.

Realized Returns
The actual returns to investors from a given investment.

Recast EBIT
Recast earnings before interest and taxes.

Recast EBITDA
Recast earnings before interest, taxes, depreciation, and amortization.

Recourse Factoring
The factor establishes how long it will wait to be paid until the accounts receivable reverts back to the client.

Red Herring
A preliminary registration statement describing the issue (the IPO) and prospects of the company that must be filed with the SEC or provincial securities commission.

Redeemable
Preferred stock that can be redeemed by the issuer at a specified price.

Registration Rights
Rights that govern the how a company goes public, who pays the cost associated with the process, and how many times it can file an IPO.

Registration Statement
Legal document filed with the SEC to register securities for public offering.

Regulation
The attempt to bring the market under the control of an authority.

Regulation A
The securities regulation that exempts small public offerings, those valued at less than $5 million, from most registration requirements with the SEC.

Regulation A+
An SEC regulation that allows companies to raise up to $50MM from both accredited and non-accredited investors. Companies that do this are called a Mini-IPO.

Regulation D
A series of six rules, Rules 501-506, establishing transactional exemptions from the registration requirements of the 1933 Act.

Related Party Transaction
An interaction between two parties, one of whom can exercise control or significant influence over the operating policies of the other. A special relationship may exist, e.g. a corporation and a major shareholder.

Replacement Cost New
The current cost of a similar new property having the nearest equivalent utility to the property being valued.

Report Date
The date conclusions are transmitted to the client.

Reporting Unit
In impaired goodwill, an operating division for which management has reviewed and assessed performance.

Repurchase Agreements
Buy/Sell agreement in which an existing entity buys a business interest from an exiting party.

Reserve
The invoice amount minus the advance plus the fee, which a factor holds until it rebates the client.

Residual Value
Value remaining in equipment after lease term has expired.

Restricted Stock Studies
Examine the issuance of restricted common stock of companies with actively traded public shares.

Restrictive Covenants
Provisions that place constraints on the operations of borrowers, such as restrictions on working capital, fixed assets, future borrowing, and payment of dividend.

Retained Earnings
Profits of the business that have not been paid out to the owners as of the balance sheet date.

Retention Plan
The plan by the acquirer to retain key personnel of the target firm post-acquisition.

Return on Capital Employed (ROCE)
A common measure of Capital Efficiency. Defined as EBIT / (Total Assets - Current Liabilities).

Return on Equity (ROE)
Measure of the overall efficiency of the firm in managing its total investments in assets and in generating a return to stockholders.

Return on Invested Capital (ROIC)
A measure of a company's capital efficiency. Defined as (net income - dividends) / (long-term debt + current portion of long-term debt + shareholders equity + capitalized lease obligations - cash - net assets of discontinued operations).

Revenue Ruling 59-60
U.S. Treasury Department ruling that outlines procedures for determining fair market value of private companies.

Reverse Merger
A private company goes public by purchasing a public company shell, then using that shell to acquire the original private company.

Revolver
A loan that can be drawn down and repaid.

Right of First Refusal
As a buy/sell provision, this right states an owner must offer to sell his shares to other owners before offering them to outsiders.

Risk
Degree of uncertainty of return on an asset. Often defined as the standard deviation of the return on total investment.

Risk Rating
System used by banks to determine a company's risk profile.

Risk-free Rate
The rate earned on a riskless asset. Technically not measurable, but in practice, US Treasury securities such as the 10-year treasury bond are used as a proxy for the risk-free rate.

ROA
Return on assets.

Roll-Up
Simultaneous consolidation and initial public offering.

Rule 504
A business using this Reg. D offering can raise a maximum of $1 million less the total dollar amount of securities sold during the preceding twelve month period under Rule 504.

Rule 505
This Reg. D offering may not exceed $5 million less the total dollar amount of securities sold during the preceding twelve month period under Rule 504, Rule 505 or Section 3(b) of the Act.

Rule 506
This Reg. D offering provides an exemption for limited offers and sales without regard to the dollar amount of the offering.

Rule of Thumb
A mathematical relationship between or among variables based on experience, observation, hearsay, or a combination of these, usually applicable to a specific industry.

Run Rate
The financial performance of a company if current results are extrapolated over a certain period of time.

Russian Roulette
Buy/Sell agreement in which the exiting party sets a share price for the stock and a period. If the stock is not bought by existing owners in the period, they may offer the exiting party their shareholdings at the originally stated price.

Safe Harbor Rule
SEC Rule 147, which allows companies to raise money without registering as a public company as long as they are incorporated, do business, and solicit investors all within a single US state.

Sale-Leaseback
Sale of an existing asset to a financial institution that then leases it back to the user.

Salvage Value
Scrap value of plant and equipment.

Sarbanes-Oxley
The Sarbanes-Oxley Act of 2002. Also called Sarbox or SOX. Expanded compliance requirements and penalties for boards of directors, management and public accountants as a response to the accounting fraud scandals at Enron and Worldcom.

SBIC
Small business investment company.

Schilt Risk Premium Matrix
Determines the discount rate by adding a risk-free rate with a premium that is associated with different levels of risk.

SCOR
Small Corporate Offering Registration. An "IPO-Lite" available under Reg A with reduced documentation and disclosures.

Second Lien Debt

Debt that is subordinate to senior debt. If the case of bankruptcy, the senior debt is paid first, then the second lien debt, which is often called mezzanine debt.

Secondary Market

The exchange or over-the-counter market where shares are traded after the initial offering.

Secured Debt

Debt that, in the even of default, has first claim on specified assets.

Securities & Exchange Commission (SEC)

Federal agency that regulates U.S. financial markets.

Securities Act of 1933

Requires companies offering securities to the public to be registered with the US Government.

Securities Act of 1934

Established the Securities & Exchange Commission (SEC) and regulates the secondary markets or exchanges.

Securitization

The process of creating a passthrough, such as the mortgage pass-through security, by which the pooled assets become standard securities backed by those assets. Also, refers to the replacement of non-marketable loans and/or cash flows provided by financial intermediaries with negotiable securities issued in the public capital markets.

Security Interest

The right of the creditor to take property or a portion of property offered as security.

Seed Stage

Funding during the idea stage of a company. This funding generally comes from the founder, angels, or family and friends.

Self-Canceling Installment Note (SCIN)
Note that terminates upon some event, usually the death of the payee.

Seller Financing
The seller of a business provides financing to the buyer for the transaction.

Selling Memorandum
Document that disseminates information to potential buyers during an auction.

Senior Debt
Debt that, in the even of a bankruptcy, must be repaid before subordinated debt receives any payment.

Senior Debt Lending Multiple
The ratio of senior debt to EBITDA

Seniority
The order of repayment. In the even of a bankruptcy, senior debt must be repaid before subordinated debt.

Series A
Typically this first round of venture capital funding for a firm. Follows angel or seed stage.

Shared Control Value
Level where no block of ownership has more than 50% of the shares.

Shareholder Agreement
Agreement that sets the terms by which shareholders deal with each other.

Shareholders' Equity
A company's total assets minus total liabilities, or a company's net worth.

Shares
Certificates or book entries representing ownership in a corporation or similar entity.

Shell Company
Existing public company in a reverse merger.

Should-Be-Private Company
Company whose costs of being public outweigh its benefits.

SIC
Abbreviated for Standard Industrial Classifications. Each 4-digit code represents a unique business activity.

Simple Interest
Interest computed on principle alone, as opposed to compound interest which includes accrued interest in the calculation.

Single Life Annuity
Private annuity whose payments stop with the death of the seller.

Size Premium
The amount that investors are compensated for assuming diversifiable or company specific risk.

Skin-In-The-Game
In private equity, refers to the general partner of a fund investing its own money in the fund as a limited partner. This shows alignment with the interests of the investors.

Small Business Administration (SBA)
Government organization that provides financial, technical, and management assistance to help Americans start, run, and grow their businesses.

Small Business Investment Company (SBIC)
Government-sponsored entity that invests in small businesses.

Sole Proprietorship
A business owned by a single individual.

Specialty Lessors
Lessors that specialize in an industry or with certain types of equipment

Specific Industry Return
The average expected return for investors in companies within a certain industry.

Specific Investor Return
An acquirer's expected rate of return.

Spin-Off
When a large enterprise takes one of its divisions and makes it a stand-alone company.

Sponsored Transaction
A private capital market deal that has a financial sponsor in the lead position.

Stages of Investment
These stages enable equity providers to match the appropriate funding source with the capital need, creating efficiency in the capital allocation process. The stages are: seed stage, start-up stage, early stage, expansion stage, and later stage.

Stakeholders
All parties that have an interest, financial or otherwise, in a firm. Includes stockholders, creditors, bondholders, employees, customers, management, the community, and the government.

Standard Deviation
A statistical measure of a probability distribution measuring the degree to which a specific value in a probability distribution varies from the expected return or value.

Standard of Value
The identification of the type of value being utilized in a specific engagement.

Startup Stage
The new venture is operational, but may not yet have revenue.

Stated Interest Rate
Interest rate before applying the "terms cost".

Stock Appreciation Rights
Rights granted to employees to receive a benefit equal to the appreciation of a given number of shares over a specified period.

Stock Exchanges
Formal organizations, approved and regulated by the Securities & Exchange Commission (SEC), that are made up of members that use the facilities to exchange certain common stocks.

Stock Gifts
Transference of stock to a family member.

Stock Market
Also called the equity market, the market for trading equities.

Stock Option
Right to buy a certain number of shares in the company at a fixed price for a certain number of years. See Call Option.

Stockholder
Holder of equity shares in a firm.

Strategic Buyer
An acquirer that intends to keep the new company as part of its long-term strategy.

Strategic Combinations
Synergies that arise from strategic motives.

Strategic Control Value
Value of 100% of the company based on strategic or synergistic considerations.

Strike Price
The stated price per share for which underlying stock may be purchased (in the case of a call) or sold (in the case of a put) by the option holder upon exercise of the option contract.

Structural Capital
The hardware, software, databases, organizational structure, and everything else of organizational capability that supports employee productivity.

Structured Debt
Debt that has been customized for the buyer, often by incorporating unusual options.

Sub-Chapter S Corporation
A business that has the limited-liability attributes of a corporation but taxation, is treated as a partnership.

Subordinated Debt
Debt over which senior debt takes priority.

Subordination
Process that determines which layer of debt has priority in a bankruptcy.

Succession Plan
The founder's plan to eventually replace the founding senior management team with professionals.

Sunk Costs
Costs that have been incurred and cannot be reversed.

Supermajority
Provision in a company's charter requiring a majority of, say, 80% of shareholders to approve certain changes, such as a merger.

Swap
An arrangement whereby two companies lend to each other on different terms, e.g. in different currencies, and/or at different interest rates, fixed or floating.

Swap Rates
Rate agreed upon between two parties exchanging short-term payments for long-term payments.

Symmetrical Information
Parties in an exchange have access to the same information.

Syndication
The co-investment of different capital providers in a single company.

Synergistic Buyer
The strategic acquirer in a synergistic relationship. See Strategic Buyer.

Synergy
The increase in performance of the combined firm over what the two firms are expected to accomplish as independent companies.

Systematic Risk
The risk common to all securities that cannot be eliminated through diversification. When using the capital asset pricing model systematic risk is measured by beta.

Tag Along Rights
Entitlement of minority stakeholder to join a transaction if the majority chooses to sell its stake.

Tangible asset
An asset whose value depends on particular physical properties.

Target
Company sought by an acquirer.

Taxable Gifts
Gifts not exempt from taxation.

Technical Know How
Proficiency in computers and/or other forms of applicable technology.

Term Loan
Loan typically used to finance fixed-asset purchases.

Term Sheet
Document that outlines the tenets of a deal and serves as the basis for its legal drafting.

Terminal Value
The value as of the end of the discrete projection period in a discounted benefit stream model.

Termination Fee
Penalty paid to the acquiror if the target backs out of the deal. See Breakup Fee.

Terms Cost
Cost of a financing beyond the stated interest rate.

Tie-Break Director
Director appointed by partners to settle a decision in the event of a deadlock.

Time Value of Money
The concept that money available today is worth more than that same amount in the future.

Trade Credit
Credit granted by a firm to another firm for the purchase of goods or services.

Trade Secrets
Any proprietary technology not generally known in the trade.

Trademarks
Protected word, name, symbol, or device or combination thereof used by a company to identify and distinguish its goods from competitors. Carries a term of 10 years, renewable upon expiration.

Tranche
Is the piece, portion or slice of a deal or structured financing. Tranches have distinctive features which for economic or legal purposes must be financially engineered or structured in order to conform to prevailing requirements.

Treasury Stock
Common stock that has been repurchased by the company and held in the company's treasury.

Triggering Events
Events that activate a buy/sell agreement.

True Lease
Lease in which the lessor takes the risk of ownership and, as owner, is entitled to the benefits of ownership, such as tax benefits.

Two-Step Auction
Each step of the selling process is staged using deadlines.

Unadjusted Indicated Value
Value conclusion before any discounts or premiums are applied.

Undersubscribed
At the end of the fundraising phase of an investment fund, the fundraising goal is has not been achieved.

Underwriter
Securities firm that purchases securities from the issuer and then sells them in an underwritten public offering.

Uniform Commercial Code (UCC)
When a lender receives a personal guarantee from a borrower, the lender will often file a UCC lien against the individual assets of the borrower, which prevents the borrower from selling those assets while the debt is still in place.

Unitranche Debt
The combination of senior debt and mezzanine debt into a single loan package.

Unlevered Beta
The beta reflecting the risk of a firm if it had a capital structure without debt.

Unsecured Debt
Debt that does not identify specific assets that can be taken over by the debtholder.

Unsystematic Risk
The portion of total risk specific to an individual security that can be avoided through diversification. See Idiosyncratic Risk or Company-Specific Risk

Unused Line Fee
A negotiated fee that is some percentage of the difference between a facility amount and the funded amount.

Upper Middle Market
Businesses with annual revenues between $500MM and $1B.

USPAP
Uniform Standards of Professional Appraisal Practice.

Utility Patents
Patent on an invention or any certifiable improvement of an existing product. Carry a term of 20 years from date of application.

Valuation
The act or process of determining the value of a business, business ownership interest, security, or intangible asset.

Valuation Approach
A general way of determining a value indication of a business, business ownership interest, security, or intangible asset using one or more valuation methods.

Valuation Date
The specific point in time as of which the valuator's opinion of value applies (also referred to as "Effective Date" or "Appraisal Date").

Valuation Method
Within approaches, a specific way to determine value.

Value Conclusion
Ultimate value after all adjustments are applied.

Variable Interest Rate
The variable percentage paid for borrowing money.

Venture Capital
Money provided by professionals who invest alongside management in early to expansion stage companies that have potential to develop rapidly.

Venture Debt
Lessors that provide equipment to startup and early stage companies.

Vertical Integration
Merger in which one firm acquires another firm that is in the same industry but at another position in the supply chain.

Vesting
The "earning" of stock by founders or key employees upon continued employment.

Visitation
Right of investors to attend board meetings and meet with management on a periodic basis.

Volcker Rule
A rule under Dodd-Frank that limits proprietary trading of securities by banks.

Voting Rights
The rights to vote on matters that are put to a vote of security holders.

Warrant
A security entitling the holder to buy a proportionate amount of stock at some specified future date at a specified price, usually one higher than current market.

Wash-Out Round
This is a venture capital funding round for a company that is not doing well, so the share price is very low (a down round) which means that the new infusion of capital results in a high level of dilution of the stakes of the investors in prior rounds. Also known as burn-out round or a cram-down round.

Waterfall
The order in which gains flow to the various stakeholders in an investment fund.

Wealth Replacement Trust
Trust that owns a life insurance policy payable upon death to the trust to received by the beneficiary.

Weighted Average Antidilution
Form of antidilution protection that prevents the value of shareholdings from being reduced by later share sales at lower prices.

Weighted Cost of Capital (WACC)
The expected return on a portfolio of all a firm's equity and debt securities. Used as a hurdle rate for capital investment.

Working Capital
Current assets minus current liabilities (excluding short-term debt).

Write-down
Decreasing the book value of an asset if its book value is overstated compared to current market values.

Yardstick Approach
Valuation method that makes a comparison with similar businesses to determine if there is a difference in the level of the plaintiff's performance after a business interruption.

NOTES

NOTES

NOTES

CPSIA information can be obtained
at www.ICGtesting.com
Printed in the USA
FSHW022221220821
84224FS